LEGENDS OF WARFARE

AVIATION

Bell 47/H-13 Sioux Helicopter

Military and Civilian Use, 1946 to the Present

WAYNE MUTZA

Schiffer Publishing Ltd

4880 Lower Valley Road • Atglen, PA 19310

Other Schiffer Books by the Author:
Green Hornets: The History of the U.S. Air Force 20th Special Operations Squadron (978-0-7643-2779-7)
Loach! The Story of the H-6/Model 500 Helicopter (978-0-7643-2343-0)

Designed by Justin Watkinson
Type set in Impact/Minion Pro/Univers LT Std

ISBN: 978-0-7643-5376-5
Printed in China

Published by Schiffer Publishing, Ltd.
4880 Lower Valley Road
Atglen, PA 19310
Phone: (610) 593-1777; Fax: (610) 593-2002
E-mail: Info@schifferbooks.com
www.schifferbooks.com

For our complete selection of fine books on this and related subjects, please visit our website at www.schifferbooks.com. You may also write for a free catalog.

This book may be purchased from the publisher.
Please try your bookstore first.

We are always looking for people to write books on new and related subjects. If you have an idea for a book, please contact us at proposals@schifferbooks.com.

Schiffer Publishing's titles are available at special discounts for bulk purchases for sales promotions or premiums. Special editions, including personalized covers, corporate imprints, and excerpts can be created in large quantities for special needs. For more information, contact the publisher.

Acknowledgments

This book would not have been possible without the kind and generous assistance of the following: Don Brabec; Jose Carlos Cardosa; Robert F. Dorr; Larry Ford; Harry (Ned) Gilliand, Jr.; Trooper Edward S. Gronlund, Pennsylvania State Police Aviation Section; Bob Leder; Terry Love; Lennart Lundh; Jim Mara; Pat McCollam; Stephen Miller; Dale Mutza; Wal Nelowkin; Eugene S. Nock; Andres Ramirez; Emiel Sloot; Steve Williams; and Ray Wilhite.

Contents

Introduction

Anyone with even a general interest in aviation finds it difficult not to admire the iconic Model 47 helicopter and the fascinating history of Bell Aircraft Corporation and its people. The open lattice framework of the helicopter's tail boom and its bubble canopy became its recognizable trademark.

A true renaissance man, Gill Robb Wilson, in the May 3, 1946 issue of the *New York Herald Tribune* wrote about the helicopter: "In all history no single instrument of transportation ever gave so much early promise or had a more limitless potential … so fantastically bright is the possibility of the helicopter, and so rich in basic advantage that the temptation is strong to abjure patience and throw the machine into premature markets." Wilson wrote this two months after the Civil Aeronautics Administration issued the first commercial license for a helicopter, Bell's Model 47.

Lawrence D. Bell, one of the men responsible for the Model 47's success, wrote in the August 1948 issue of *American Helicopter*: "The day will come when every Coast Guard Station has at its disposal one or more helicopters to increase the certainty of rescue under virtually any condition. The day will come when the Red Cross will dispatch by helicopter its first-call aid to disaster areas. As a vehicle to bring supplies or medical care to the stricken, or to evacuate the sick and the hurt to shelter and care the helicopter has work of tremendous importance. During its two years of existence, the helicopter has exerted a powerful impact upon the life of our world as a new tool, to perform a hundred tasks. Already its accomplishments give substance to the dreams of Daedalus, da Vinci, and all others who sought this kind of flight."

Other inventors and philosophers shared Bell's dream and took risks, including Arthur M. Young who during the 1920s challenged his inventiveness. Young set off down the road of success—and failure—testing flying models to solve the pervasive problem of rotor control and stability. After a decade of research, he invented the stabilizer bar, which allowed the rotor to operate independently of the mast. At the first demonstration of his invention at Bell Aircraft Corporation in September 1941, Young met Larry Bell. Instantly, they hit it off as a team and agreed that Young and his assistant Bartram Kelly would build two prototypes. Bell was busy turning out P-39 fighters for the war effort, while his small helicopter team forged ahead with three Model 30 rotary-wing craft in a rented garage in Gardenville, New York. The trio evolved into the Model 47, which was rolled out on December 8, 1945. Encouraged by its success, and with war production at a standstill, Bell turned to helicopter production. It was a wise decision, for the Model 47, in a wide variety of configurations, would remain in production for nearly twenty-eight years.

After the Korean War, the demand for helicopters soared as the machine once viewed as a foolhardy contraption proved itself in combat. Interest in both commercial and military applications grew, and it would reaffirm its value many times over. Larry Bell did not live long enough to realize the full extent of his immeasurable faith in the helicopter, its accomplishments, and the thousands of lives they saved. As of this writing, more than 1,000 Bell 47s are still flying worldwide.

Members of the Gardenville group ride aboard Model 30, Ship 3 in 1945, to test its weight lifting capability. Bell pilot Joe Mashman is at the controls, while inventor Arthur Young stands opposite, facing the camera. Above his head is his patented stabilizer bar, which relied upon gyroscopic principles to ensure flying stability. Ship 3 was the first of Bell's long line of Model 47s to be fit with the signature bubble canopy. *Courtesy of Bell Helicopter*

The Model 30 Ship 1A is displayed at the Smithsonian Institution in its final configuration, wearing wheel pants and a small windshield. Prior to donation to the Smithsonian in 1964, Ship 1A traded its center fuselage wheel for a nose wheel. Overall yellow was standard livery for Bell's test helicopters. *Author's Collection*

The first Bell helicopter was re-designated Ship 1A after a rebuild following a crash in September 1943. Here, during a test flight, Ship 1A shows off its new metal covering and redesigned landing gear. *Courtesy of Bell Helicopter*

Bell's first helicopter, named "Genevieve," is rolled out of the Gardenville plant wearing new blue coverings and wheels that replaced tubular legs. The plant, a former automobile facility with garage, was obtained to concentrate on development of the helicopter, separate from Bell's fixed-wing production. *Author's Collection*

In May 1944, Bell test pilot Floyd W. Carlson made the first indoor flight with a helicopter at the request of the Civil Air Patrol, when he flew Model 30 Ship 2 inside Buffalo, New York's 65th Regiment Armory. Ship 2 was the aircraft most used by Bell as a demonstrator. Carlson was Bell's first helicopter test pilot, having transferred to the helicopter project in 1942 from his post as fighter test pilot. During the late 1940s, he was Bell's top salesman, flying demonstrations and giving rides to nearly 2,000 people. *Author's Collection*

At Niagara Falls on March 8, 1946, the day Bell was awarded the first commercial helicopter license, Floyd Carlson demonstrates the Model 47's stability with hands off the controls. Registration NC-1H was one of two, the first having been destroyed in an accident. This NC-1H was later destroyed in a landing accident while in service with Bell's training school. *Author's Collection*

Bell officials examine the bubble canopy, which was formed by injecting air pressure into heated Plexiglas. Larry Bell resisted the enclosure, which became the Model 47's most recognizable feature. Besides offering protection from the elements, the canopy was found to improve performance and visibility. Inventor of Bell's helicopter, Arthur Young, kneeling at lower left, ponders his bubble enclosure. *Author's Collection*

CHAPTER 1
The Commercial Model 47

When Bell Aircraft Corporation entered the new field of rotary-wing aviation during the late 1940s, little interest was shown by the post-war military. Since the small number of military helicopters used mainly for rescue were Sikorsky types, Bell focused on the commercial market.

Even before the third experimental Model 30 was completed, Larry Bell envisioned an all-metal, streamlined, five-place machine as the helicopter of the future. Bell's associates did not share his view of the Model 42's success in the unproven commercial helicopter market. Although the Model 42 proved a mechanical nightmare, Larry Bell remained convinced that his company's future rested with the helicopter, specifically, the less fanciful, more practical Model 47.

One of the first successful applications of the Model 47 was agricultural work. Its ability to fly low and slow, hover, weave around terrain features, and blow product downward made it ideally suited for spraying, dusting, and fogging. Commercial sales were slow, with most of the Model 47s sold as single units to charter companies, corporations, flying schools, and crop dusters. To maximize use of their aircraft, early operators modified and updated their helicopters as new equipment became available.

Persistent in his efforts to devise new ways to showcase his helicopters' abilities, Larry Bell kept his demonstration aircraft on the move worldwide. He exploited peacetime use of helicopters with a number of achievements, which included record-breaking flights and establishing a list of "firsts." Still, helicopters remained relatively unproven, expensive, and seemingly difficult to learn to fly. Bell addressed the latter by immediately establishing a flying school, and enticing non-pilots with a helicopter designed with automobile-like features. The concept spawned Bell's first production model, the 47B, which featured an enclosed cabin with an automobile-type windshield and doors. A total of seventy-eight Model 47Bs were built, which included thirty-three 47B-3s specially designed for agricultural work. Lawrence Bell stated in the August 1948 issue of *American Helicopter* magazine: "Among the most spectacular uses of the helicopter was the assignment of a fleet of twelve 47B3 machines to Argentina to fight a locust plague in 1947. Working in two-ship teams, the helicopter applied 5,000 to 6,000 pounds of commercial formulations daily and secured 98% control to save millions of dollars of crops."

Billed as "The Helicopter of the Future," Bell's Model 42 was an ambitious aircraft for its time. Having been designed more as an airplane, however, spelled the demise of the streamlined, all-metal craft. Three passengers sat behind the pilot and copilot seats. Its 450 hp Pratt & Whitney, nine-cylinder Wasp Junior radial engine was cooled by a large air intake at the base of the rotor mast. The aviation world in 1946 was not receptive to such an aircraft, and only three Model 42s were built, none of which have survived. This Model 42 poses in front of Bell's Niagara Falls plant. *Courtesy of Bell Helicopter*

On December 4, 1947, Bell announced its new general utility helicopter model, the 47D, featuring a convertible canopy. The first machine went to Armstrong-Flint Helicopter Company, which was expanding on the West Coast. The 47D could be equipped with a variety of accessories, including those required for night flying. Its quadricycle landing gear, which came with parking brakes, was interchangeable with float gear.

Following closely behind in 1949 was the Model 47D-1, which, according to Bell's corporate news release, was "… stripped for action, ready to go to work." Stripping included tail boom covering, cowlings, and non-essentials. Heavy work was possible with a 200 hp Air-Cooled Motors engine, an improved transmission, and lighter, more versatile skid landing gear. The 47D-1 had a useful load of nearly 1,000 pounds.

Helping to introduce Bell's helicopter line was New England Helicopter Service, Inc. of Rhode Island, which was billed as, "the oldest helicopter company in the world." Various other markets took note and sales began to climb.

Canada's Carl Agar of Okanagan Helicopters is credited with pioneering the use of helicopters in mountainous regions. Okanagan opened its doors in April 1947, and took delivery of its first 47B-3 in August. First to put the 47B-3 to work, earlier that year, was Skyways of Winnipeg, Canada. By the mid-1950s, Okanagan had grown into the largest commercial helicopter operation in the world, with Bell 47s leading its fleet.

As interest in the helicopter grew, Bell 47s amassed hours performing a variety of tasks. Beginning in 1949, Helicopter Air Services, Inc. handled Chicago's airmail service, with six Model 47s flying more than one million accident-free miles by 1952. One year later, Sabena Belgian Airlines began a similar service in Europe with nine Model 47s. News agencies across the globe found the Model 47 useful. The first US newspaper to own a helicopter was Portland, Oregon's *The Journal*, which operated a Model 47B for news and photo coverage. The film industry followed suit after Hollywood director Nicholas Ray's 1947 groundbreaking use of helicopters to film action scenes and others never before viewed from a helicopter's perspective.

By 1948, the Model 47 had gained acceptance by the oil industry as a valuable asset in the search for natural resources beneath the earth's surface. Although the industry explored many uses for the helicopter, such as offshore operations and pipeline patrol, Bell concentrated on geophysical exploration. The first use of helicopters offshore was at the request of Kerr-McGee and Humble Oil, prompting Bell to form Petroleum Bell Helicopters Co., with surplus LSTs serving as the first offshore landing platforms. When ownership later changed, the Bell name was deleted and the company became Petroleum Helicopters, Inc. (PHI). By 1960, PHI was flying thirty-eight Bell 47s.

Much of the credit for the success of rotary-wing aviation in Arctic regions goes to early pioneers such as Lou Leavitt, America's first licensed helicopter pilot, who supervised the helicopter division of Alaska Airlines when it purchased two 47Bs and a 47D in 1949. James Ricklefs, founder of Rick Helicopters, took over Alaska Airlines' fleet of twenty-two Bell 47s in 1951. His intense involvement with mapping survey work, for a time, made Rick Helicopters the largest commercial helicopter company in the world, with twenty-six Bell 47s on inventory. Close behind was Keystone Helicopter Corp. of Philadelphia with twenty-five Bell 47s. Other major operators by 1960 were Aero Copters, Inc. of Seattle, flying fourteen Bell 47s; Calicopters with ten; and the Canadian firms Spartan Air Service having nineteen, and Associated Helicopters with thirteen Bell 47s.

With few military orders at the end of World War II, Bell Aircraft Corporation focused on the commercial market for its helicopters. The Model 30 displaying the ease of delivering mail was one of countless demonstrations that Larry Bell insisted would generate public interest. At his insistence, the second proof-of-concept Model 30 seen here (registered NX 41868), featured side-by-side seating. *Courtesy of Bell Helicopter*

Undeniably, the effectiveness of the helicopter during the Korean War shaped its success in commercial aviation. Veteran pilots started charter services and more operators opened new fronts for the helicopter. The tasks performed by Bell's family of Model 47s seemed limited only by the user's imagination. Within its first ten years of helicopter production, Bell delivered 500 commercial Model 47s to fifty-five nations, accounting for more than two million flight hours.

A newfound sense of value based on the helicopter's proven abilities, which generated a surge of interest by the military, meant expanding the Model 47 line. When President Larry Bell decided to separate the helicopter operation from the older, fixed-wing operation to achieve its full potential, the new Fort Worth facility became the birthplace of the Model 47 that exceeded all production totals. When Bell welcomed guests to the formal opening of the new Texas Division in June 1952, he said, "This is only the beginning for helicopters, their services and conveniences." Although he added, "There still is much to be done in designing, engineering and production," the first model designed and developed in the new facility embodied all the lessons learned from earlier models. Introduced in 1953, the Model 47G was testament to the ability of engineers and their skill in applying the vast amount of operational experience of Model 47s to create a star performer. The 47G offered more range, maneuverability, and stability than previous models. The G model differed outwardly in having "saddle bag" fuel tanks holding forty gallons of fuel, which increased range 38%, and a synchronized elevator linked to the cyclic, allowing greater center-of-gravity range and improved stability. An adjustable battery rack eliminated the previous requirement to shift the battery between tail boom and nose positions to maintain balance as loads changed. Powering the 47G was a six-cylinder Franklin air-cooled engine rated at 200 brake horsepower at 3,100 rpm.

Bell pilot Floyd Carlson tests float landing gear on the Model 47B prototype No. 2, registered NX 41967 in 1947. Inflatable floats were laced to steel tubes that were fastened to struts for wheels. *Author's Collection*

Ann Shaw, the first woman to become licensed as a helicopter pilot, began working for New York's Metropolitan Aviation Corporation, flying sightseeing trips in a 47B around Manhattan. The 47B had a gross weight of 2,150 pounds, a useful load of 594 pounds, and flew at 85 mph. *Courtesy of Smithsonian Institution*

During the twelve years following the 47G's debut, the type served as the basis for continual upgrades resulting in more than a dozen variants ranging from a single machine to hundreds. Two variants, the 47G-2 and the 47G-3B-1, enjoyed production runs exceeding 300. The latter was designed to overcome altitude, temperature, and humidity restrictions encountered by piston-engine helicopters. Having achieved success with utilitarian helicopters, Bell designers and engineers decided to try their hand at a high end version of the Model 47. The result in 1955, was the 47H "Bellairus," which was a deluxe version of the 47G, featuring the same dimensions. Marketed as an executive transport, the all-metal, streamlined 47H featured a soundproof cabin, all-leather interior, and luggage compartment in the tail boom. Accommodations for pilot and only two passengers impeded its marketability, and only thirty-three were built. The Bellairus did, however, serve as a major stepping stone between the 47G "Trooper" series and the 47J "Ranger" series of helicopters, the first of which went into production in 1955.

Resembling somewhat an enlarged Bellairus, the 47J had a larger cabin that accommodated four passengers. As had occurred with the 47G line, the 47J served as the basis for continued improvements resulting in a number of model designations. Both the 47G and 47J families of helicopters quickly gained worldwide popularity, with hundreds produced under license by Great Britain's Westland, Italy's Agusta, and Kawasaki in Japan. To stimulate commercial sales, Bell in 1956 sent a 47J on a tour of fifteen Central and South American countries and Cuba, covering 17,000 miles.

The first practical use of the helicopter for motion pictures was accomplished by RKO Studios for filming "Your Red Wagon," released in 1948. Scenes shot from the red-painted, gyro-stabilized Bell 47B of Armstrong-Flint Helicopter allowed shots impossible by other methods. Here, stars of the film Cathy O'Donnell and Farley Granger, are filmed in August 1947 by cameraman Paul Ivano. Harry Armstrong and Knute Flint were considered pioneers in the field of commercial helicopters. *Author's Collection*

Actor Melvyn Douglas poses with the Model 47B used in the production of the film "Mr. Blandings Builds his Dream House." This helicopter also advertises the aircraft's role in first class mail service, and noted movie stunt pilot Paul Mantz. Mantz Air Services was among twenty-two commercial users of Bell helicopters in 1948. This 47B, registered NC112B, had a landing light installed in the nose. *Author's Collection*

Capitalizing on the Model 47's success were manufacturers that developed new designs based on the Model 47's airframe. Carson of Pennsylvania produced a number of conversion kits, and had designed a cabin to convert the Model 47 to a four-seater, called the "Super C-4." Continental Copters of Fort Worth developed its "Tomcat" as a single-seat agricultural helicopter based on the 47G-2. A similar agricultural spin-off from Texas Helicopters was labeled the M-74 "Wasp," and a two-place version called the M-79T "Hornet." Joe Soloy's experience with underpowered helicopters in the wilds of Alaska and Canada led him during the late 1970s to form a company to replace the unreliable piston engine with light and powerful Allison 250-C series gas turbine engines. The Allison 250 was battle-proven, having powered Hughes OH-6A Cayuses during the Vietnam War. Soloy's conversions of eleven Model 47G variants, called "Soloy Lama," quickly gained favor with helicopter operators that worked in hot and high conditions.

Production of the Model 47J series ceased in 1966, but not before both J and G models had set records for speed, distance, and altitude, most having occurred during early 1961. Turbine power came into vogue, diminishing the demand for piston powered helicopters, and, subsequently, Model 47 production. Outnumbering military versions, more than 2,600 commercial Model 47s had rolled off the assembly line during a twenty-eight-year run.

When British European Airways formed its Experimental Helicopter Unit in July 1947, a Bell demonstrator and two 47B-3s were imported for the fleet. One of them, seen here being evaluated with spray equipment, was named "Sir Balin." The 47B-3 "Roadster" carried 400 pounds of product in two removable side-hoppers. *Author's Collection*

Shortly after founding Okanagan Helicopters Ltd., Carl Agar brought to Canada one of the nation's first commercial helicopters, seen here in 1947 dusting orchards at Penticton, British Columbia. The 47B-3 was Okanagan's first of many Bell Model 47s operated throughout Canada. Later outfitted with skid landing gear, this aircraft was flown throughout rugged mountain ranges for topographical survey work. *Author's Collection*

Bell's third-built 47B, registered NC5H, served as the company demonstrator until 1951 when it was purchased by Chicago Seaplane Base. Aerialist Marilyn Rich, billed as the "Original Helicopter Girl," performs with the aircraft to promote the 1951 National Air Races. In 1957, NC5H went to the Energy Equipment Company of Monticello, Iowa. Dr. Carol Voss started AgRotors, Inc. in February 1958, with the purchase of NC5H, which flew until 1972. *Author's Collection*

The Model 47D was Bell's fourth variant in the basic 47 series which debuted in 1947. Its cabin was enclosed to provide year-round service, plus passenger comfort. A split bubble canopy allowed removal of the roadster windshield and attachment of the top half of the bubble, with doors included. Within a few years, most of the earlier 47B-3s were brought up to 47D standards, which included skid landing gear. An Air-Cooled Motors six-cylinder 178 hp engine gave the 47D a gross weight of 2,200 pounds, a top speed of 95 mph, and a service ceiling of 11,500 feet. This aircraft (c/n 24) later went to Canadian registry. *Courtesy of Bell Helicopter*

Bell's Model 47D was the first of the design to be produced in large numbers. This early example, seen at the Buffalo, New York plant, tested float landing gear. Although float gear varied according to time frame and manufacturer, basically they were neoprene-coated nylon fabric bags divided into cells with separate filler valves. They added approximately sixty pounds to the aircraft. *Courtesy of Bell Helicopter*

Metal cowlings and fabric covered tail boom changed dramatically the appearance of early Model 47s. This 47B-3 was registered NX 131B, indicating its experimental status. *Author's Collection*

Skid gear was offered as an option with the 47D-1. This model was easily distinguished from the D model in having an exposed tail boom frame, requiring a ventral fin and a tail rotor guard. The battery visible within the latticework of the tail boom would be mounted on the rack forward of the instrument pedestal if only the pilot was aboard. The dual location was necessary to maintain weight balance. This 47D-1 (N78980-c/n 480) with agricultural dusting gear is seen in April 1952. *Author's Collection*

A mix of Model 47B, 47D, and 47D-1s await delivery at Bell's Buffalo, New York plant. Visible attached to five of the 47Ds are cargo carriers that added twenty cubic feet of cargo space to each aircraft, or 400 pounds of cargo. *Author's Collection*

The registration of this Model 47G was carried forward from Okanagan's first helicopter, a 47B-3. The company was one of the Canadian pioneers in the use of Bell helicopters. By 1965, Okanagan owned twenty-one Bell 47s, most of which were painted in the firm's striking orange and black livery. *Author's Collection*

Mountainside platforms were built by Okanagan during the 1950s and 1960s to serve as landing sites during major powerline construction projects. Pilots that flew the routes over rugged terrain in severe weather were called "Platform Pilots." *Author's Collection*

The Model 47G was Bell's first helicopter designed and developed entirely at the Fort Worth facility after the company's move there in 1951. The G model spawned more variants than any other model 47, and it was the most widely produced. Noteworthy features were dual gravity-feed fuel tanks that increased range by 38%, ground handling wheels incorporated into aluminum skids, and a bench seat that accommodated three persons. A synchronized elevator expanded center-of-gravity limits to the extent the battery no longer had to be relocated for weight balance. The white area atop the bubble canopy often was applied at the factory, and sometimes in the field with white shoe polish. The disc not only reduced sun glare, at night it reduced glare from lights on the ground that reflected onto the bubble, thereby disorienting pilots. *Courtesy of Bell Helicopter*

For nearly seventy years, the Canadian utility Ontario Hydro, now named Hydro One Networks, Inc., operated helicopters, mainly for powerline maintenance in rugged terrain. The firm began its helicopter fleet in 1949 with a Bell 47D-1, and by the 1970s, had upgraded to Model 47Js such as this example at Toronto's Malton Airport in 1971. Ontario Hydro is the first utility to use helicopters in North America. *Courtesy of Grady Cates Collection*

Osterman's Aero was the first commercial operator outside the US, and a true pioneer in Sweden. Beginning in 1947, the firm introduced helicopters to a number of services. Osterman's was the first international firm to purchase the Bell 47. This 47J was built in 1958, and served the Swedish Air Ambulance Service beginning in 1964. The 47J was one of more than a dozen Model 47 types operated by Osterman's. Small skis helped this 47J operate in snow conditions during its seventeen years in Sweden. *Courtesy of Lars Soldeus*

Billed as the first television series written about helicopters, "Whirlybirds" starred Kenneth Toby and Craig Hill as two pilots operating a charter service. A total of 111 episodes were filmed between 1954 and 1958, and featured a Bell 47D and a 47J. This crude facsimile of a Bell 47 served as a stationary filming prop for close-ups. *Author's Collection*

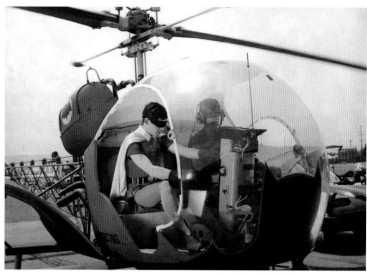

A 47G-3B-1 was leased by National Helicopter Service to star as the "Batcopter" in the 1966 film "Batman." Unlike other novel "Bat" vehicles, the Batcopter was not used in the 1960s TV series due to its cost. Another drawback was canvas wings fastened to a tubular frame that reduced power by fifty percent. The same aircraft (N3079G) was used for the film "Lassie Come Home," and by CBS News. Nockair Helicopter, Inc. purchased the Bell, which it modernized, including the Batcopter scheme. *Author's Collection*

As Suburban Propane Gas Corp. expanded to the eastern US, its use of helicopters also increased and included this Model 47G seen over New York City. *Author's Collection*

Certified for export by the CAA, the 47G quickly became popular worldwide. Heliswiss, the oldest helicopter firm in Switzerland, was founded in Berne in April 1953, and began operations with a handful of 47Gs. Unusual on this 47G in 1960, is a partial tail boom covering. *Author's Collection*

This 47D-1 served aboard ice patrol ship HMS *Protector* (A146) during 1956 and 1957, as part of the Falkland Islands and Dependencies Aerial Survey Expedition (FIDASE) to map Antarctica's Anagram Islands. *Author's Collection*

John D. Silva, chief engineer for Los Angeles KTLA-TV in 1958, outfitted a leased Bell 47 to create the "Telecopter," which essentially was a flying television studio. It placed Channel 5 at the forefront of live aerial news coverage and added another first to the Model 47's long list of accomplishments. *Author's Collection*

Los Angeles KTLA Channel 5 upgraded to a Model 47J seen here displayed with equipment of KMPC News, which included a 47H. *Author's Collection*

A Bell 47G-4A (N8182J) of Petroleum Helicopters, Inc. (PHI) on Ship Shoal 209 in 1975. Early in the Model 47's career, its role in the petroleum industry was deemed so vital to Bell's commercial interests that PHI was founded as Petroleum Bell. *Courtesy of Robert Coveny*

Texas Senator John L. McClellan departs Little Rock, Arkansas in July 1954, while seeking re-election to a third term. His "Campaign Buggy" was a 47G of Rod More Aviation of Corpus Christi, Texas. Also in political circles, President Lyndon Johnson had a long-term relationship with Bell helicopters. During his 1948 Senate campaign, Congressman Johnson used a Bell 47D to reach rural voters across the expanse of Texas. In 1957, as Senate Majority Leader, Johnson rolled out the 2,000th model, a 47J, from the Hurst plant. *Courtesy of Library of Congress*

Chesapeake and Potomac Airways, Inc. used Model 47Js for scheduled flights between Washington National Airport, Baltimore's Pier 4, and Andrews Air Force Base, Maryland. Here, Baltimore Mayor Thomas D'Alesandro, Jr. flies the service in July 1957. *Author's Collection*

The Protection Civile, as it was known until it became Securite Civile in 1976, is a civil defense agency of the French government. For more than fifty years, the agency has operated helicopters, including this Model 47G. Aircraft are overall yellow with the international civil defense symbol. The G's fuel tanks were mounted next to the rotor mast, the center-of-gravity, eliminating load restrictions. *Author's Collection*

The first Model 47H went to President Larry Bell for his personal use. The second machine went to Columbia's President Gustavo Rojas Pinilla. Bell's 47H "Bellairus" (N996B) was painted blue and gold and wore his initials on the cabin door. It is now displayed at Niagara Aerospace Museum. Built in 1955, the 47H accommodated a pilot and two passengers. As far back as the days of the Model 30, Bell insisted that at least one example have dual seating so that he could fly as a passenger. *Courtesy of Bell Helicopter*

The Model 47H demonstrator (N960B) which was built in 1954. Common with most Model 47s, cowlings were seldom used or they were screened, for engine cooling. *Courtesy of Bell Helicopter*

The wide assortment of helicopters flown by New York Airways included a pair of Model 47Hs. Periodically, they were equipped with float landing gear. In 1957, when Bell had on its drafting boards a design for a three-turbine, twenty-five-passenger helicopter based on its HSL-1 anti-submarine helicopter, New York Airways President Robert L. Cummings, Jr. advocated a cooperative undertaking between commercial and military interests for a premium, yet cost-effective helicopter. *Courtesy of Terry Love*

As the helicopter evolved, new or improved equipment created a growing market for specialized use of the helicopter. Sling-loading bucket containers was a specialized task, first for seeding, fertilizing, and pesticide application, and later for firefighting. A 47G-3B-1 of Western Helicopters sling-loads a bucket mounting a power spreader. *Courtesy of Bell Helicopter*

Production of the Model 47G-3B began in 1961. The G-3B's turbo-supercharged 260 hp Lycoming engine set it apart from the G-3. It had its military equivalent in the H-13S, 265 of which were purchased for the US Army. Kawasaki built 210 G-3Bs as the KH-4. *Courtesy of Bell Helicopter*

Very high skid gear allowed this 47G to carry a magnetometer, which normally saw use with US Navy sub-hunter aircraft. Only marginal success was achieved with the helicopter-mounted AN/ASQ-10, since its components had to be separated as far as possible to avoid machine interference. Since the late 1940s, Bell was keen on the use of its Model 47s for geographical exploration, including gravity metering, seismic, and radar surveys. Bell operated a fleet of helicopters under contract to oil interests to explore otherwise impassable regions, mainly in the south and southwest US. *Courtesy of Harold Troxell*

During the mid-1950s, Hawk Helicopters of Corpus Christi, Texas, contracted with Shell Oil Co. for offshore work. This 47G, outfitted for over-water work with rescue litters and float gear, was named "Sea Hawk." *Courtesy of Shell Oil Company*

Washington National Airport was home to a number of VIP helicopter transports including this immaculate 47J-2A Ranger (N1155W), seen here in July 1970. The official seal on the cabin door states, "Member of Congress – United States of America." Visible on the interior cabin firewall is a portrait of John F. Kennedy. *Courtesy of Steve Williams*

Fresh from the factory, a Model 47G-5A is test flown prior to delivery to Mobil Oil. This model was a spinoff of the G-5. Both were powered by a 260 hp Lycoming, however, the G-5A had seating for three and an eleven-inch wider cabin. The G-5A's gross weight was 2,850 pounds. Fully loaded, its fuel capacity of fifty-seven gallons gave it a range of 240 miles. The G-5A's maximum speed was 113 mph. *Courtesy of Bell Helicopter*

A wider cabin and increased fuel capacity resulted in the 47G-3B-1 introduced in 1963. A total of 337 of this model were built. Older style skid gear was popular with operators who found them useful for mounting equipment such as litters, cargo carriers, etc. The fuel tanks of this demonstrator display the word "Turbo" in reference to the 270 hp turbo-supercharged Lycoming engine that differentiated the 47G-3B-1 from the G-3B. This livery was standard for Bell deliveries. *Courtesy of Bell Helicopter*

This 47J-2A Ranger at Hong Kong Harbor in 1974, was used for sightseeing. The prefix "VR-H" identifies aircraft registered in Hong Kong. *Courtesy of Wal Nelowkin*

A Model 47G-5 of Wilbare Ellis, an agricultural firm, departs Mesa del Ray Airport, California in July 2010. Eighty-gallon capacity tanks on both sides of the aircraft allowed sprayers to cover more than fourteen acres per minute at 60 mph. Modern spray-equipped Model 47s typically used a single fuel tank to allow more product to be carried. *Courtesy of Steve Nation*

Unsurprisingly, the Nock brothers, pilot Eugene and aerialist Michelangelo, bill themselves "The Nerveless Nocks." The "Helicopter Trapeze" is but one of the Nock family's many thrill shows preformed worldwide. The Nocks pride themselves in maintaining their Model 47G-3B-1 in show condition, which includes chromed engine parts. Nockair Helicopters is based at Longboat Key, Florida. *Courtesy of Eugene Nock*

Based on the H-13H, this 1979 OH-13H/M74A, owned by Hendrickson Flying Service Inc. of Rochelle, Illinois, displays its versatility doing agricultural work in July 2014. From 1976 to 1981, Texas Helicopter Corp. built forty M74s in various models based on the Bell 47. *Courtesy of Paul Meier*

This Model 47G is in the final steps of conversion to turbine power by Soloy Corporation of Olympia, Washington. The large tubular device is an oil cooler assembly. Large fuel tanks hold fifty-seven gallons. The Soloy/Bell with Allison 250-C20B turbine engine has a maximum gross weight of 3,200 pounds, and a ceiling of 16,000 feet. *Courtesy of Soloy Corporation*

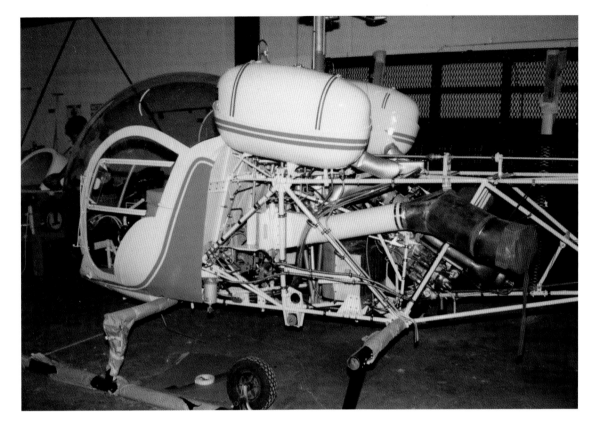

Despite resistance by Bell, Soloy in September 1978, won approval to rebuild Model 47s, with the major portion of the rebuild involving replacement of piston engines with turbine engines. Soloy's rebirth of the Model 47 bolstered the resurgence of interest in the type by offering operators a reliable workhorse 47G. This 47G works as an agricultural sprayer, a common application of Soloy Bells. *Courtesy of Soloy Corporation*

The Bel Air Sport Coupe with Body by Fisher. Every window of every Chevrolet is Safety Plate Glass.

YOUR PRIDE WILL PERK UP *whenever you're seen in your* '58 CHEVROLET. *One look at those low, wind-whisked lines and you know you're bound to be noticed. And you'll find still more to be proud of in the quick, sure way Chevy responds to your touch.*

Sure as it's a Chevy, you're going to be looked at when you drive this good-looker. Don't be surprised if you even hear a soft whistle of approval now and then. There's just something about Chevy's low, straining-at-the-bit beauty that makes people sit up and take notice.

The way this Chevrolet *moves* is something to be admired, too. Its quick-sprinting power, for example, and the reassuring way it keeps its poise, even on sudden dips and curves.

Another big reason you'll be

prouder of a Chevy is that it's the only honest-to-goodness *new* car in the low-price field. There's a new X-built Safety-Girder frame . . . new Turbo-Thrust V8* . . . new longer, lower Body by Fisher . . . a choice of new standard Full Coil suspension or a real air ride.* Cars just don't come any newer—or nicer—than this one.

Stop by your Chevrolet dealer's real soon. What he's selling is high on pride but low on price. . . . Chevrolet Division of General Motors, Detroit 2, Michigan.   *Optional at extra cost.*

CHEVROLET

Graphic promotion of the helicopter, especially Bells, was widespread during the 1950s. One can't help but notice the Model 47B-3 agricultural sprayer the artist added to this car ad in 1958. *Author's Collection*

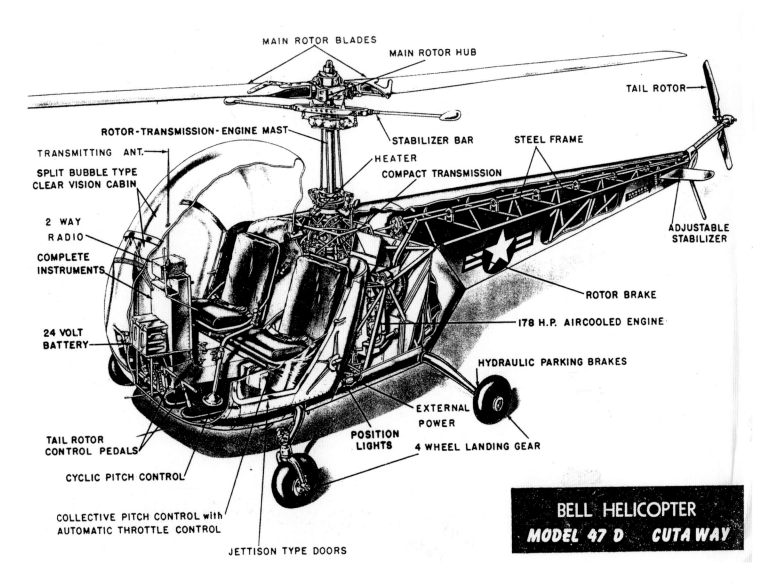

MAIN ROTOR BLADES

MAIN ROTOR HUB

TAIL ROTOR

ROTOR-TRANSMISSION-ENGINE MAST

STABILIZER BAR

STEEL FRAME

TRANSMITTING ANT.

HEATER

COMPACT TRANSMISSION

SPLIT BUBBLE TYPE
CLEAR VISION CABIN

ADJUSTABLE
STABILIZER

2 WAY
RADIO

COMPLETE
INSTRUMENTS

ROTOR BRAKE

178 H.P. AIRCOOLED ENGINE

24 VOLT
BATTERY

HYDRAULIC PARKING BRAKES

EXTERNAL
POWER

TAIL ROTOR
CONTROL PEDALS

POSITION
LIGHTS

4 WHEEL LANDING GEAR

CYCLIC PITCH CONTROL

COLLECTIVE PITCH CONTROL with
AUTOMATIC THROTTLE CONTROL

JETTISON TYPE DOORS

BELL HELICOPTER
MODEL 47 D   CUTAWAY

This Model 47D cutaway drawing was one of countless graphics included in Bell advertisement material about 1950. *Author's Collection*

CHAPTER 2
US Military Service

Mindful of its ample experience with early Sikorsky helicopters during World War II, the army in 1946, ordered twenty-eight Model 47As when Bell was nearing civil certification. These were the first Bell production machines, which the army labeled the YR-13. Three were earmarked for the Army Air Force (AAF), fifteen for the Army Ground Force (AGF), and ten were allocated to the US Navy, which labeled them HTL-1s. The AAF trio was modified for cold weather tests in Alaska and re-designated YR-13As. The fifteen army machines underwent testing, eventually ending up at the Army Air Force helicopter training site at San Marcos, Texas, which had been established in 1946. In 1948, Bell received an army order for sixty-five H-13Bs, which were similar to the YR-13, but featured a more powerful 200 hp Franklin engine and split canopy. The army, in keeping with its policy of naming aircraft for American Indian tribes, in 1949, dubbed its H-13 the "Sioux." More commonly called simply, "The Bell," its primary duties were observation, utility, medical evacuation, and training.

The navy established Helicopter Utility Squadron One (HU-1) in April 1948, followed by HU-2 one year later to coincide with delivery of a dozen HTL-2s, the navy equivalent of the Model 47D. Designation HTL stood for Helicopter, Training, Light, which satisfied the navy's search for a rotary-wing trainer. Helicopter Training Unit One (HTU-1) was established in December 1950, and within one year, had on its inventory nearly sixty helicopters, most of which were Bell HTL-4s and -5s for training navy and marine pilots. All students started in the HTL, which was the easiest to fly among the school's three types, which included the Piasecki tandem-rotor HUP, and Kaman's HTK with intermeshing rotors.

One for the record books—which was sure to stay out of the record books—is an account told by an HTU-1 instructor about one of his colleagues, a test pilot attached to the maintenance section. "George," he starts, "was a likeable bastard, with a lot of guts and maybe a little short on good sense. George always talked about the possibility of doing a loop with the HTL. He told most of the pilots on the base that some day he was going to loop a Bell. One morning, an instructor came running into the ready room saying, 'George is up there trying to loop a Bell; he's going to bust his ass!' We all ran out to see. Sure as hell, George not only looped it once, but twice. The 'wheels' heard about it and George got called before the skipper. The skipper tried to let him off the hook by

Bell's Model 54 was a beefed-up military derivative of the Model 47. The all-metal, four-place liaison and observation craft was requested by the US Army Air Force in 1946. Given military designation XR-15, the helicopter used the Model 47's rotor system powered by a 275 hp Continental engine. Three XR-15s, serial numbers 46-530/532, were built but no production contracts followed. *Author's Collection*

saying, 'George, you really only did a half-ass split-S, didn't you?' George replied, 'No, Captain, I did two complete loops and they were good ones too.' George didn't get reprimanded, but the word was posted: 'Pilots will not, repeat, will not do acrobatic maneuvers such as loops, rolls, split-Ss, etc. in helicopters.'"

The navy took delivery of 183 HTL models, up to the HTL-7, the last of which arrived in 1969. From 1955 to 1959, thirty-four HUL variants joined the navy, with navy Bells remaining on squadron rosters until mid-1973. The H-13 held the title of the navy's primary helicopter trainer at Naval Air Station (NAS) Ellyson Field, Pensacola, Florida until 1969.

Marine Corps aviation officially began with the commissioning of Helicopter Squadron One (HMX-1) in December 1947. Reluctant to replace their fixed-wing observation aircraft, marine leaders relented after evaluating an HTL loaned by the navy. A pair of HTLs was added to the Marine Corps inventory during 1948, and by the start of the Korean War, the Marines had fourteen HTLs. To address a shortage of helicopters in the war zone, ten navy HTL-4s were turned over to Marine Observation Squadron Six (VMO-6). The Marine experience with HTLs ended in 1955 with five HTL-5s still in service.

The US Coast Guard has long made use of helicopters. Besides assigning helicopters to ocean and inland waters icebreakers, they flew shore and harbor patrol, law enforcement, and search and rescue missions. The first Bell helicopters that wore coast guard markings were a pair diverted from the navy's original batch of ten HTL-1s. Under President Truman's

1950 Magnuson Act, which charged the coast guard with US port security, in July 1951 a coast guard port security helicopter detachment was established for New York City. Three orange-painted, float-equipped HTL-5s were assigned to Brooklyn Air Station. Until 1960, the trio flew daily patrols accumulating record numbers of flight hours for helicopters, so many, in fact, that jerry cans filled with fuel were carried, and oversized fuel tanks later replaced standard twenty-nine-gallon tanks. The coast guard later acquired two HTL-7s for icebreaker duty, and two HUL-1Gs outfitted for search and rescue in the Bering Sea. HTL-7s in 1962 were re-designated TH-13Ns and HUL-1Gs became HH-13Qs.

The US Air Force utilized the H-13 in various functions, however, it served mainly as a trainer until 1958. After a civil defense drill in the mid-1950s, during which cabinet members in a helicopter arrived at a bunker before President Eisenhower riding in his limousine, the search was on for a presidential helicopter. The Secret Service resisted strongly, insisting that the president fly in fixed-wing, multi-engine aircraft only. Regardless, the search ended at Bell, which customized two H-13Js, one to carry the president to be flown by combat-seasoned Air Force Maj. Joseph Barrett, and the other flown by Capt. Lawrence Cummings to accompany the president carrying Eisenhower's physician and a Secret Service agent. After Eisenhower's reign, the job of transporting presidents went to Army and Marine Corps helicopter detachments, flying much larger helicopters, much to the relief of the Secret Service.

When war broke out in Korea, the army possessed sixty-three H-13s. That number skyrocketed to more than 600 by the end of 1954. The first H-13s arrived in Vietnam in 1962, and by 1972, the army world inventory counted more than 1,100 H-13s in models E, G, H, S, and the TH-13T. Arguably, the most famous among them were Sioux Warriors, the experimentally-armed H-13s that defied the skeptics and evolved into the Aeroscouts of the Vietnam War.

Although the interest of and the demand for helicopters rose sharply after its success in Korea, its use as a weapons platform was not quickly embraced. That military application would endure the growing pains suffered by development of the helicopter itself. Credit for the first bonafide use of Bell's Model 47 in the armed role goes to the French, who gave teeth to their Bell 47s with rockets and machine guns for the eight-year Algerian war beginning in 1954; US military leaders watched closely, since capitalizing on the helicopter's potential for warfare was a siren's call. When US Army Col. Jay Vanderpool was appointed by Brig. Gen. Carl Hutton, commander of the Army Aviation School, to research the helicopter's capabilities, Vanderpool put arming the helicopter at the top of his list. Research for the helicopter was being done and helicopter doctrine was being written at various army commands, and a new concept called "Sky Cav" included experimentation with armed helicopters.

After an H-13 static-fired machine guns and rockets in July 1956, blueprints were drawn up for a helicopter strike force, which met fierce opposition. But "Vanderpool's Fools" persevered and Aerial Combat Reconnaissance (ACR) became reality. The field opened wide, resulting in innumerable evaluations of armed helicopters, with Bell's H-13 a major participant.

Although the H-13 in the Aeroscout role did a credible job in Vietnam, it was limited in the amount of weaponry it could take to the enemy. However, its involvement with armament tests prior to the war, coupled with the Aeroscout experience, served as the foundation for the success of future armed helicopters.

The first military Model 47A, the YR-13, serial no. 46-227. *Author's Collection*

As either a trophy or as food, a caribou arrives aboard navy icebreaker USS *Edisto* (AGB 89) lashed to the float of an HTL-1 (BuNo. 122458). The helicopter wears the code of Helicopter Development Squadron Three (VX-3), which was decommissioned in April 1948 to form HU-1 and HU-2. The newly commissioned *Edisto* was on its first summer cruise near Canada's Ellesmere Island.
Courtesy of US Navy

This is one of two HTL-1s allocated for the coast guard from the navy's initial order for ten machines. It began life as a YR-13 with Army Air Force serial number 46-254 and served the coast guard until 1955. Next to the screened engine compartment cowling is the fuel tank access cowling. The triangular panel aft of that was called the strut access cowling. One of the HTL-1s flew mainly from the icebreaker *Mackinaw* on the Great Lakes, while the other was aboard cutter *Eastwind* in Greenland and Ellesmere Island in the far north of Canada. Both were lost in crashes. *Courtesy of US Coast Guard*

An HTL-2 (BuNo. 122959) of Helicopter Utility Squadron Two (HU-2) puts on a display at its home base NAS Lakehurst, New Jersey, in October 1948. The squadron shared the blimp hangar with Blimp Patrol Squadron Fourteen (ZP-14). *Courtesy of US Navy*

This is the first of twelve HTL-2s delivered to the navy (BuNo. 122952) serving with HU-1 on an icebreaker off Alaska in 1950. On the fuselage is squadron code "UP," followed by the aircraft number. *Courtesy of Ned Gilliand Collection*

Bureau Number 122963 was the last of twelve HTL-2s built for the US Navy. The frame piece with support rods on the forward canopy permitted the top portion of the canopy to be removed for the "convertible" option. Early navy HTLs were painted Gloss Sea Blue with a yellow empennage. The HTL-2's gross weight was 2,100 pounds. *Courtesy of US Navy*

The first helicopter assigned to Ft. Belvoir, Virginia, was this H-13B (s/n 48-828). The post aviation section later replaced the wheels with skid landing gear. The front wheels of early model 47s were self-castering. Army H-13Bs were painted dull aluminum.
Courtesy of US Army

Bell's commercial Model 47D-1 was the basis for the navy's HTL-3 and -4. Only nine HTL-3s went to the navy before being superseded by the HTL-4, which featured an improved transmission. Seen here is the first HTL-3 built (BuNo. 124561) undergoing flight tests at NAS Patuxent River, Maryland in August 1950. The HTL, with the main rotor in the position shown here, measured twenty-seven feet, four inches in length. Its wheel track was six feet, eight inches, and its height to the top of the rotor head was nine feet.
Courtesy of US Navy

A tradition seemingly as old as the military itself was decorating aircraft to celebrate Christmas. This HTL-4 of Helicopter Training Unit One at NAS Pensacola, Florida, received the thorough holiday treatment in 1951.
Courtesy of Malone H. Farrar

Believed to be one of eleven Model 47 prototypes, this example possibly is a YH-13 that was reconditioned for use as an instructional airframe. It appears to be missing major components and wears later style markings. *Courtesy of US Army*

As the thirteenth H-13D built, serial no. 51-2458, left the production line with quadricycle wheeled gear, which would be replaced by skid gear. The absence of fabric tail boom covering in the D model required the addition of a ventral fin for stability. Weight and balance in the H-13D had to be monitored to stay within center-of-gravity limits for control of the aircraft. If only the pilot was aboard this H-13D, the battery would be relocated from the center tail boom to the platform forward of the pilot's legs. *Courtesy of Bell Helicopter*

Bureau Number 129970 was one of thirty-six HTL-5s built for the US Navy. A foil antenna encircles the face of the canopy. Inside the "bubble" is a VHF radio, the antenna of which projects through the Plexiglas. Also atop the radio is a receiver loop antenna. *Courtesy of Bell Helicopter*

This General Electric kit was the first armament system designed for use on helicopters. Only its four center tubes could fire 2.75-inch rockets because outer tubes were too close to the M60A machine guns. The inboard gun was mounted inverted to allow ammunition to feed properly. The kit is seen damaged due to the H-13 landing on uneven ground. *Courtesy of US Army*

Helicopter manufacturers sometimes experimented with weapons as a private venture. In 1966, Bell engineers modified this 47G-3B (OH-13S) to accommodate a machine gun fired through an opening in the canopy. The gun's travel was limited and the concept was discarded. *Courtesy of US Army*

Besides experiments with arming helicopters at various testing sites, makeshift weapons were devised by units in the field. Members of the 24th Infantry Division fabricated this grenade launcher for the H-13 in Japan in 1953. *Courtesy of US Army*

Swiss-made Oerlikon rockets and .30 cal. machine guns gave this OH-13E significant firepower. *Courtesy of US Army*

Comprising this experimental ACR kit was a pair of AN-M2 .30 cal. machine guns over a six-tube arrangement of 2.75-inch rockets. This system was tested at Ft. Rucker, Alabama, in 1957. *Courtesy of US Army*

A modified M60D machine gun was mounted to the arch skid tubes of this OH-13S (s/n 63-9212) of the Aerial Reconnaissance and Security Troop, B Troop, 3rd Squadron, 17th Cavalry at Ft. Rucker, in 1965. *Courtesy of US Army*

The XM1E1 armament kit used twin M37C .30 cal. machine guns, seen here mated with a test H-13 at Aberdeen Proving Ground in 1963. *Courtesy of US Army*

The army's Redstone Arsenal developed the two-inch Weevil rockets tested on this H-13H during 1957 and 1958. Long firing tubes were used to test dispersion patterns. Mounted above the tubes are .30 cal. machine guns. Redstone Arsenal at Huntsville, Alabama, became known as "The Rocket Capitol of the World." The rocket was named after the equally destructive boll weevil insect that plagued Alabama crops. *Courtesy of US Army*

Bell modified two H-13Hs to fire SS-10 missiles. The army took delivery of the pair in mid-1958, but by year's end, the missiles were ruled excessive for use with the H-13. The French-designed SS-11 wire-guided missile, however, was successfully used with Bell's UH-1 Huey helicopter. Although the SS-11 won approval by the US Marine Corps in 1957, its use with marine helicopters became mired in a stalemate over arming helicopters. *Courtesy of US Army*

The army's second-built TH-13T (s/n 64-17846), which became the army's primary instrument trainer. The student pilot in the right seat wears blinders that limit his vision, along with other cockpit features, to learn to fly on instruments. *Courtesy of Bell Helicopter*

The cockpit of the first of more than 400 TH-13T trainers ordered by the US Army. The tinted bubble canopy is apparent. Besides a host of avionics, the cockpit would become more crowded once operational with hooded panels for instrument flight training. *Courtesy of US Army*

Details of Model 47s often are difficult to distinguish, but this image taken by Lennart Lundh is a welcome study of the TH-13T (s/n 67-17024) at the Army Aviation Museum at Ft. Rucker, Alabama.

The TH-13T (s/n 66-8062) at Ft. Eustis, Virginia, in 1972. For more than six decades, army training aircraft have worn liberal amounts of International Orange paint, along with large, white numbers followed by a letter. The upper surfaces of rotor blades are painted with white bands.
Courtesy of Stephen Miller

This Model 47G-3B served as Bell's demonstrator. The name "GI Joe" and a caricature of a winged GI on the fuel tank reflected a large order of the type for the US Army as the H-13S. Introduced in 1961, the H-13S was powered by a turbo-supercharged 260 hp Lycoming TVO-435-25 engine. *Courtesy of Bell Helicopter*

Incorporated into the engine powering the OH-13S was an AiResearch exhaust-driven supercharger which enabled the aircraft to maintain its normal rated power up to an 18,000-foot hover ceiling. This machine (s/n 63-9072) was the first of an army order for 265 OH-13Ss, which had its commercial equivalent in the Model 47G-3B. *Courtesy of Bell Helicopter*

Although wire strike protection kits did not appear until the mid-1970s, experiments with the H-13S demonstrator speak to Bell's early recognition of the deadly mix of low-flying helicopters and wires. This cumbersome arrangement comprised projecting saw-tooth runners and three wire cutters above. Affixed to the belly of the 47G-3B named "GI Joe" is a smoke generator for flight demonstrations.
Courtesy of Ned Gilliand Collection

The HUL-1 (BuNo. 142371) poses with her squadron mates of HU-2 at NAS Lakehurst, New Jersey, in January 1957. Above the HUL-1 is a Piasecki HUP-2, and at the top a Sikorsky HO4S-3. All wore the standard for US Navy helicopters, Light Gull Gray.
Courtesy of US Navy

Helicopter detachments assigned to ships shared tight quarters with crews and equipment. Float gear was standard during cruise duty, such as those on this HUL-1 (BuNo. 143142) in 1959. Floats were two feet wide and 13½ feet in length. The engine access doors of HUL-1s typically were used only when the aircraft was parked. *Courtesy of A.D. Berkebile*

A pair of HTL-4s of HU-1 were parked close together on the crowded deck of LST 561 *Chittenden County* during Project 517, which was resupply of the Distant Early Warning (DEW) Line in the Arctic during 1955. *Courtesy of Malone H. Farrar*

The HUL-1 (BuNo. 143144) of HU-1 came to a bitter end when it caught fire and crashed on takeoff from the icebreaker *Atka* (AGB-3) on December 1, 1957. The *Atka* was one of nine US Navy ships comprising Task Force 43 in Ross Sea during Operation Deep Freeze I. The wreckage was pushed overboard. *Courtesy of US Navy*

A TH-13M (BuNo. 142386) of the US Navy Test Pilot School at NAS Patuxent River, in 1971. Designated HTL-6 prior to 1962, forty-eight of these navy trainers were delivered during the mid-1950s. They featured metal rotor blades with rotor brakes. This aircraft later went to the Royal Canadian Navy. *Courtesy of Stephen Miller*

On July 12, 1957, Dwight D. Eisenhower became the first US President to fly on board a helicopter. He seems pleased with the VH-13J custom-built by Bell for his use. His pilot, Air Force Maj. Joseph Barrett, flew B-17s in World War II, and was awarded the Silver Star during the Korean War for a helicopter rescue flight he made seventy miles behind enemy lines. Both VH-13Js were based at Washington National Airport. *Courtesy of Bell Helicopter*

The Air Force Presidential Helicopter Mission ended with Eisenhower's presidency. In 1961, the pair (s/n 57-2728/2729) was assigned to the 1001st Helicopter Squadron at Bolling Air Force Base, DC, to serve as VIP transport. This VH-13J wears the emblem of the 1254th Air Transport Wing (Special Air Missions). The designations UH-13J and VH-13J were used interchangeably. Both were retired in July 1967 and given to museums. *Courtesy of Bell Helicopter*

When presidential transport duty went to Army and Marine Corps VIP helicopter detachments during the 1960s, the VH-13Js became VIP transports with the 1001st Helicopter Squadron in the Washington, DC area. Number 57-2729 is seen here with a four-star general's placard at Andrews Air Force Base, Maryland, in August 1966. In 1969, the 1001st became the 1st Helicopter Squadron of the 89th Military Airlift Wing, still charged with VIP transport. *Courtesy of Richard Sullivan*

Although the air force was the procurement agency for army Bell H-13 helicopters, a few were acquired by the air force, mainly for training. Both H-13D and E models were used at the helicopter school until 1958, when the school was relocated to Stead Air Force Base, Nevada. For ten years, the H-13 shared the training role with the R-5, H-19, and H-21 helicopters. The H-13 was phased out due to its limited power. This well-maintained H-13E (s/n 51-13809) was assigned to Flight Test Center at Edwards Air Force Base, California until 1970. *Courtesy of Norm Taylor*

The H-13H essentially is the same helicopter as the commercial Model 47G-2. It was powered by a 260 hp Lycoming engine derated to 200 hp. It was built especially for maximum performance at high altitude and in extremely hot weather. The first two H models were delivered to Camp Rucker, Alabama, for tests in 1955. The H introduced arched skid cross tubes, although the older type remained the customer's choice for use as equipment platforms. *Courtesy of Bell Helicopter*

Details of an H-13G used for testing of stretcher platforms attached to skid cross tubes. The ARC-12 radio antenna is visible projecting through the canopy. *Courtesy of Bell Helicopter*

Cockpit of s/n 63-9072, the first OH-13S produced for the US Army. Instruments of most Model 47s were contained in a center pedestal to allow maximum visibility through the canopy. The aircraft data plate is affixed to the pedestal's lower side panel. The pilot's cyclic control rests against tail rotor foot pedals for tail rotor directional control. Immediately left of the seat is the main rotor blade pitch control for lift, which incorporates the throttle. This aircraft crashed on takeoff on March 28, 1968, while assigned to B Company, 1st Aviation Battalion in Vietnam. *Courtesy of Bell Helicopter*

During the early 1950s, three HTL-5s were operated by the coast guard's port security section in New York City. The HTL-5 was the US Navy designation for the H-13E, which was a Model 47D-1 powered by a Franklin engine and upgraded with dual controls and a third seat. The three HTL-5s (CG No. 1268/1270) carried five-gallon jerry cans filled with aviation fuel on both sides of the aircraft. The Sikorsky H-19 at right was from the air force 46th Air Rescue Squadron at Westover Air Force Base. *Author's Collection*

An HTL-3 is secured aboard Coast Guard Cutter *Northwind* during its 1955 summer cruise, in support of DEW Line operations from July to September. Helicopters normally were assigned to navy and coast guard ships, mainly for scouting and resupply. An added safety measure to negotiate the tight quarters of ships was an additional tail rotor guard installed on this HTL-3. Many World War II era ships had their seaplane catapults removed to facilitate helicopter operations. *Courtesy of US Coast Guard*

During the early 1960s, HU-4, based at NAS Lakehurst, possessed fourteen HTL-7s, along with HRS-3s and HUS-1s to provide helicopter detachments to all non-aviation ships of the Atlantic Fleet, plus Arctic and Antarctic navy and coast guard icebreakers. This HTL-7 (BuNO. 145844) is seen at Harewood, New Zealand, while assigned to USS *Atka* in 1961. *Courtesy of Jack Friell Collection*

While operating in the Bering Sea in 1955, this HTL-4 (BuNo. 128901) of HU-1 was fitted with locally-fabricated panels to retain heat in the engine compartment. *Courtesy of Tailhook Photo Service*

US Naval Reserve helicopter pilots Lt. Howard R. Downard and Ens. John W. Erlewine of HU-2 study charts while assigned to coast guard icebreaker Westwind on a five-month cruise in Arctic waters in 1955. Their inflatable life vests include shark chaser repellent and sea dye markers. Shown to good effect is the lace pattern used to secure float gear to the aircraft. *Courtesy of US Coast Guard*

Coast Guardsmen work with a new telescopic hangar aboard the cutter *Northwind* on Bering Sea patrol in June 1963. The hangar not only protects helicopters from cold weather and salt water, it allows crewmen to work in heated confines with lighting and a deluge foam system in case of fire. The aluminum retractable hangar was developed by the Canadian Ministry of Transportation. The two-place HH-13N, previously the HTL-7, was painted overall yellow. *Courtesy of US Coast Guard*

The HTL-4 replaced the HO3S-1 as the primary medevac helicopter in Korea. This HTL-4 was assigned to Marine Helicopter Squadron One (HMX-1), which was commissioned at MCAS Quantico, Virginia, on December 1, 1947. In place of litter baskets, HMX-1 HTLs sometimes carried quick-release life rafts, which were developed by navy squadron HU-2 in 1947. *Courtesy of US Navy*

An earthquake on the Greek island of Kefalonia in 1953, prompted an American rescue effort that brought together army, navy, and air force helicopters on the deck of the carrier USS *Franklin D. Roosevelt* (CVB-42). An army H-13E (s/n 51-13911) of the 7th Army in Germany, is prepared for medical evacuation, while an air force H-5H and navy HUP stand by in the background. *Author's Collection*

US Army aviation mechanic students train with an H-13E. This model's most distinguishing feature was the vertically-mounted carburetor air intake aft of the elliptical fuel tank. The tail boom structure comprised welded steel tubes. Fabric-covered tail booms of earlier models often hid cracks caused by corrosion. After two crashes of HTLs caused by corrosion in 1954, the navy grounded all HTLs. As an anti-corrosion measure, tail booms were filled with banana oil and drained. *Courtesy of US Army*

This Model 47 carried three designations during its military career. It began life as one of the last HTL-6s delivered to the US Navy. The type was re-designated TH-13M in 1962. When the Army National Guard inherited numerous H-13s and HTLs, the Florida Army National Guard took possession of this aircraft. It then became an OH-13G but retained navy bureau number 143168. It is seen here at Jacksonville, Florida, in 1971. The HTL-6 was similar to the HTL-4/-5 in having metal rotor blades, rotor brake, and improved controls. *Author's Collection*

Beginning on September 2, 1956, the first-built H-13H (s/n 55-3355) at the National Aircraft Show at Oklahoma City, was kept aloft for fifty-seven hours and fifty minutes, an unofficial world record. The feat was accomplished by ground personnel using jerry cans to fill modified fuel tanks on both sides of the aircraft. *Courtesy of US Army*

In 1948, the army added H-13 helicopters to its demonstration team. In 1951, the H-13s formed an "Army Helicopter Square Dance Team," and "Bozo the helicopter Clown." In the spirit of perpetual rivalry, the navy in 1952, formed the "Rotary Wing Angels" comprised of HTLs. Here, Bozo the Clown Helicopter performs at the Transportation Corps 12th Anniversary celebration at Panzer Kaserne, Germany, in July 1963. *Courtesy of US Army*

An OH-13H shares the flight line with its older brothers, Bell UH-1 Huey helicopters in 1968. The OH-13H (s/n 58-5376) later went to the Spanish Army. *Author's Collection*

Since limits were placed upon the number of OH-13s committed to the Vietnam War to maintain balance at US bases worldwide, others were deployed across Europe. This OH-13H at Heidelberg AAF, Germany, in the 1960s, served one of numerous aviation units of the 7th Army. *Courtesy of Jack Friell*

CHAPTER 3
Emergency Services

As the helicopter emerged, it wasn't long before personnel of firefighting, rescue, and law enforcement agencies recognized the potential of the strange machines. They saw in the helicopter the ultimate force multiplier, the most revolutionary tool in their inventory. Capitalizing on the helicopter's capabilities changed the face of emergency services, and Bell's Model 47 got in on the ground floor.

The successful marriage of the helicopter and law enforcement took place in April 1948, when the New York Police Department (NYPD) acquired its first Bell Model 47. The chopper was requested by the nation's first-rated police helicopter pilot, NYPD Officer Gus Crawford, after he was sent to Bell's training school at Buffalo, New York. Crawford said, "I used to fly Mayor O'Dwyer around in the police department's Grumman Goose. One day he asked me if there was anything I needed. 'I want a helicopter,' I answered." Not only did the NYPD helicopter fleet grow to be one of the largest among US law enforcement agencies, the department remained a loyal Bell customer.

The fire service in America boasted use of the helicopter earlier than establishment of the NYPD fleet. Experimentation by the US Army and the US Forest Service (USFS) with Sikorsky R-5s in 1945, had helped set the stage for helicopter use in fighting wildland fires. Renowned helicopter pilot Fred Bowden, along with Armstrong-Flint Helicopter Co., is credited with inaugurating use of the helicopter in fighting forest fires in 1947. That summer, the USFS requested from Bell a Model 47B (reg. N183B) to work the Bryant Fire at Angeles National Forest in southern California, marking the first full operational use of firefighting helicopters. During California's Wheeler Springs Fire in September 1948, the largest that year, helicopters were pressed into service on an even larger scale, proving their worth by delivering firefighters and supplies, and serving as a scouting platform.

In 1954, a large-scale experiment was conducted in California's San Diego area to evaluate a variety of equipment and techniques in combatting wildland fires. Called Operation Firestop, the project demonstrated the helicopter's ability to fan backfires, drop water and firefighting chemicals, and deliver supplies to firefighting crews. The term "Helitack" was coined by the US Forest Service in 1956, and by the early 1960s, the program was in full swing.

The importance of America's Civil Defense during the height of the Cold War is reflected in this pair of Model 47Hs acquired for the Office of Civil Defense (OCD). These were early research and development variants of the 47H Bellairus, which was the deluxe version of the Model 47G. A sound-proofed, leather-lined cabin accommodated a pilot and two passengers, and the metal-covered tail boom housed a luggage compartment. Adorned with OCD emblems, the Bellairus (N966B) in the foreground was the aircraft of Val Peterson, former governor of Nebraska and Leader of Civil Defense from 1953 to 1957. The other 47H (N960B) is marked as a press aircraft. Both were built in 1954, prior to introduction of the Model 47H, also called the 47H-1. *Courtesy of Bell Helicopter*

After a rash of large brush fires during the late 1950s, Los Angeles Fire Department (LAFD) officials enlisted the aid of the USFS, along with one of their own firefighters, Theodore "Bud" Nelson. Although a combat-seasoned fixed-wing pilot and experienced water bomber pilot, Nelson, after watching Bell 47s help build the Palm Springs Aerial Tramway, envisioned the helicopter as the most successful aircraft for the fire service.

With LAFD Chief William Miller's blessing, Nelson and pilot Clarence Ritchey on December 12, 1961, took delivery of a new Model 47G-3B at Bell's Fort Worth plant. After training by Bell technicians, the pair flew the aircraft to Los Angeles. Upon completion of an extensive training program, the new "Fire Bird" was placed in service on April 22, 1962. Less than one month later, Fire Bird worked at its first blaze, the Tuna Canyon Fire.

The primary function of the LAFD helicopter was to serve as an aerial command post at large fires. From above, the field commander could "read" the fire and direct operations accordingly.

Unfortunately, Fire Bird was destroyed on June 23, 1964, after hitting power lines during a training flight, killing both pilots. That year, the LAFD acquired its second helicopter, a Bell Model 47J-2A, registered N73272. Recognizing the value of the helicopter, Los Angeles Mayor Sam Yorty made extensive use of the aircraft as an executive transport. A Bell 47G-3B-1 was soon added to the aviation section to serve as a helitack firefighter and rescue platform.

Concurrent with formation of the LAFD Helicopter Unit, the Los Angeles County Fire Department also began a helicopter unit with Bell 47s. To maximize the helitack role of their chopper, department personnel developed a 100-gallon fixed water-dropping tank. The LAFD quickly followed suit in fitting the tank to its pair of Model 47G-3B-1s.

After turbine-powered helicopters became all the rage during the late 1960s, Los Angeles city and county fire departments joined the trend, again choosing Bell-made helicopters.

Beginning in 1971, more Bell 47s appeared in California skies after San Diego County Sheriff John Duffy spearheaded a program that provided aerial law enforcement support to all public safety agencies in the San Diego area. By 1971, ASTREA (Aerial Support to Regional Enforcement Agencies), named after the Greek goddess of justice, was formed. San Diego's County Sheriff's Department acquired three Bell 47s, which proved so successful, especially at search and rescue in rugged, remote areas, that three more Bell 47s were obtained.

Regardless the type of emergency service organization, or area that it served, the Bell Model 47 typically was its first helicopter. Even the federal director of the Office of Civil Defense during the Cold War encouraged municipalities to acquire helicopters since only the helicopter could provide the mobility necessary following A-bomb attacks. Common in both small and large communities were helicopters operated jointly by fire and police departments. This arrangement not only saved cost, it fostered cooperation between departments whose members often worked hand-in-hand, providing services that often overlapped. The City of Chicago was a prime example, whose fire and police departments operated jointly both Bell 47s and rescue boats in the Air-Sea Rescue Unit.

Some agencies found it easier on their budgets to lease helicopters. For crew training, emergency service organizations often relied upon civilian agencies that already were well-versed in the Model 47. For example:

When the Pennsylvania State Police initiated its Helicopter Patrol Project in 1968, the department took advantage of Bell's Flight Transition and Field Maintenance School at Fort Worth to qualify six pilots. Troopers who were assigned as mechanic/observers attended Bell's Model 47G-4A maintenance course, Lycoming Division's Aircraft Engine Course, or the maintenance program offered by Ag-Rotors, Inc. at Gettysburg, Pennsylvania. Some troopers attended Ag-Rotors Flight Training School.

Both 47G-4As were delivered in mid-March equipped with detachable Bell stokes baskets and NiteSun searchlights. Operating as patrol vehicles, the pair, within their first nine months of service, responded to 368 incidents, the majority of which involved searches for persons, crime surveillance, and traffic incidents.

Taken during the fire at the Shasta-Trinity National Forest in August 1955, this photo was used by Bell Helicopter Company to illustrate the Model 47's usefulness in carrying fire hose across terrain inaccessible by ground vehicle. Included in the picture are other elements vital to fighting forest fires: fire crews, vehicles, pack horses, bulldozer, and smoke jumper. *Courtesy of Bell Helicopter*

True to its reputation for being a leader in public service, Seattle acquired this Bell Model 47G-2 for its police department in 1960. Float gear was essential since the aircraft could quickly respond to water emergencies. Antennas of early radios projected through the bubble canopy. The 47G-2 was powered by a 250 hp Lycoming engine derated to 200 hp. This was the first Model 47 equipped with metal main and tail rotor blades. *Author's Collection*

Throughout most of its history the NYPD Aviation Unit was equipped with Bell helicopters. This early Model 47 carries a rescuer on a rope ladder. Nearby is a boat of the Harbor Division, which worked closely with the Aviation Unit. *Courtesy of Fred Freeman*

The New York City Police Department acquired its first helicopter in 1948. The department's aviation unit had been activated in 1929 with fixed-wing aircraft. In 1954, it became an all-Bell helicopter unit. With the exception of four Agusta Westland A119s operated early in the twenty-first century, the unit has flown Bell helicopters throughout its history. This Model 47D-1 was one of six helicopters flown by the NYPD Aviation Unit. With the city's extensive waterways, floats and litters were standard equipment. *Author's Collection*

Los Angeles Fire Chief William L. Miller cleared the way for the department's first helicopter. Chief Engineer Miller (at right) looks over the Model 47G-3B "Fire Bird," with Fire Commissioner Henry O'Bryant on January 30, 1962. Pilot "Bud" Nelson is in the cockpit. The aircraft later was repainted in the LAFD scheme and a loudspeaker system was added. *Courtesy of Pat McCollam*

The LAFD helicopter "Fire Bird" was powered by a 260 hp Lycoming six-cylinder engine with turbo-supercharger. With a maximum gross weight of 2,850 pounds, Fire Bird could carry three persons, including pilot. A forty-one-gallon fuel capacity allowed aloft time of two hours, forty-five minutes at normal power settings. Electronic equipment included radios to communicate on all LAFD and LA County fire frequencies. *Author's Collection*

When commercial versions of the famed Bell Huey became available during the 1970s, the LAFD retired its first Model 47G-3B-1. The department's 1963 vintage Model 47 served into the twenty-first century, although on a part-time basis. The aircraft is seen here in 2000, equipped with a fixed-water-drop tank. *Courtesy of Pat McCollam*

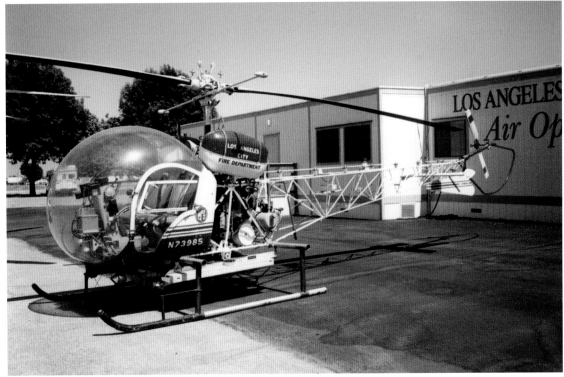

The Honolulu, Hawaii Fire and Police Departments operated this Model 47G cooperatively, a common arrangement in many communities. Registered N47379, the 47G is seen here in 1969. *Courtesy of Nick Williams*

Prior to forming its Helicopter Patrol Project, the Pennsylvania State Police conducted a pilot program with this Model 47J-2A acquired in June 1968. The aircraft's protruded cabin door was a Bell modification made available to carry two stretchers crosswise in the cabin. No record exists of this helicopter entering service. *Courtesy of Trooper Ed Gronlund, Pennsylvania State Police Aviation Section*

Pennsylvania State Police Bell 47 mechanic/observers attended repair and maintenance programs conducted by Bell Helicopter, Lycoming, and Ag-Rotors, Inc. These troopers trained at the Ag-Rotors six-week course, which began at the company's Gettysburg site in 1958. *Courtesy of Trooper Ed Gronlund, Pennsylvania State Police Aviation Section*

Registered N1413W, the Model 47G-4A was one of two delivered to the Pennsylvania State Police Aviation Section in March 1969. This aircraft was based at the Washington County Airport, while N1412W operated from Middletown's Olmsted Airport. The green and white aircraft were delivered with Bell litter carrier kits and NiteSun searchlights. N1413W crashed after two years of service, and 1412W completed nearly five years of service before it was lost in a crash. *Courtesy of Trooper Ed Gronlund, Pennsylvania State Police Aviation Section*

Florida's Metropolitan Dade County Public Safety Department operated this 47G-3B-2 (N8185J), which left the production line in 1972. It was powered by a Lycoming TV O-435 engine. *Author's Collection*

Emblems of both Radio Station WMAL and the Metropolitan Police Department identify the dual role of this attractive Model 47J at Washington, DC, in 1970. Based at Washington National Airport, the traffic reporting helicopter was flown by a Metropolitan Police Department pilot. The name "Queenie" appears in small print on the forward door frame. *Courtesy of Steve Williams*

Wearing the standard scheme for Bell deliveries, this 47G-4A served the City of Chicago as a cooperative effort by the fire and police departments. Registered N225FD, the Bell is seen here at Chicago's Meigs Field, in August 1970. This helicopter later operated under two owners in France and then in Madagascar. *Courtesy of Steve Williams*

Built in 1968, this 47G-4A served Chicago public safety in updated livery, which included a broad engine panel that served as a signboard. Loudspeakers were added to both sides of the aircraft, which often flew with a scuba diver aboard. *Courtesy of Steve Williams*

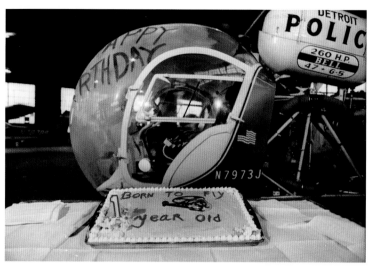

Like a number of police departments across the US, Detroit exploited the attributes of the Model 47, flying this 47G-5 on drug raids, chasing fleeing robbers, and numerous police tasks. So pleased were department personnel with the performance of their Bell, they threw a party for their teammate. In 1974, when Detroit's Police Aviation Section added four helicopters, each patrolled an assigned sector of the city. *Author's Collection*

Prior to the advent of turbine-powered helicopters, Model 47s were popular with law enforcement agencies, which found the Bell easy to fly and maintain, cost effective, and durable. Seen here in February 1970, this 47G-3B-2 was operated by the Denver, Colorado Police Department. *Author's Collection*

This Model 47G-2 of the Detroit Police Department crashed when its rotors struck a pole while landing in tight quarters in June 1983. The pilot was slightly injured and a passenger was unhurt. Helicopter pilots agree that landings in urban settings merit extra caution. *Author's Collection*

In 1948, the New York Police Department introduced the helicopter to police operations, beginning with Bell Model 47D-1 helicopters. In 1954, the NYPD Aviation Section became an all-helicopter unit. The department was consistent with Bell helicopters, having upgraded to 47Js, such as this example seen in 1967. *Courtesy of Police Department, City of New York*

Numerous law enforcement agencies took advantage of the availability of surplus military helicopters during the 1970s. This well-maintained Model 47 of the Minnesota Highway Patrol began life as an army TH-13T (s/n 64-17880). Later it was acquired by the Delaware State Police Aviation Unit. *Courtesy of Charles Mayer*

While it's unlikely that this dramatic 1955 magazine cover accurately depicts operations with Bell 47s during wildland fires, it illustrates the awareness of the helicopter's versatility during a period when sales of the Model 47 soared. *Author's Collection*

About eighty percent of all the helicopters flown during the conflict were Bells, and they account for an equal percentage of all the wounded evacuated by air. Not to be overlooked is the number of missions flown by US Marine Corps Bell HTLs of Marine Observation Squadron Six (VMO-6). In December 1950, the squadron received two HTL-3s and three HTL-4s. Marine aviators in Korea found the -3's landing gear and tail boom construction unsatisfactory for rugged terrain, favoring instead the HTL-4's open tail boom and skid gear, which accommodated enclosed litters. Marine HTL-4s flew most patients to hospital ships *Repose* or *Consolation*, the latter eventually having a landing pad installed. Statistics for 1952 show the result of VMO-6's commitment to round-the-clock evacuation of front-line casualties: of a total of 2,672 evacuations, 361 were flown at night. To provide a link between forward and rear positions, VMO-6 HTL-4s often were used to lay wire; crews could lay wire at the rate of nearly one mile per minute. Marine Observation Squadrons One and Two took delivery of a small number of HTL-4s and HTL-5s in 1951, but they did not see combat in Korea.

Seldom mentioned in historical annals is the participation of US Navy Bell helicopters in the Korean War.

When Bell officials heard from US Marines that US forces in Korea were facing Russian-built T-34 tanks, they obtained the best anti-tank weapon available, a bazooka. The launcher was installed on a model 47D-1 (N237B) at Naval Air Development Center, Johnsville, Pennsylvania, for firing tests by Marine Helicopter Squadron One (HMX-1) in August 1951. A blast shield was added later to protect the engine area. Although successful, the bazooka was shot down for fear that it gave the enemy valid reason to shoot down helicopters, including those carrying wounded. *Courtesy of Bell Helicopter*

In December 1950, Capt. Albert C. Sebourn (left) helps demonstrate an enclosed litter he devised to protect patients from the elements. Sebourn, who commanded the 2nd Helicopter Detachment when it arrived with H-13Ds in November 1950, evacuated more than 1,500 soldiers in ten months. Within the first month of becoming operational in Korea, the detachment evacuated more than 500 wounded. *Courtesy of US Army*

Although navy helicopter detachments aboard ships used mainly Sikorsky HO3S-1s—which had their equivalent in the air force H-5 rescue helicopter—a small number of HTLs also served. Helicopter Utility Squadron One (HU-1) and HU-2 were formed on April 1, 1948, from the decommissioning of Helicopter Development Squadron Three (VX-3). The squadron had been established on July 1, 1946, at Floyd Bennett Field, NAS New York, to follow up US Coast Guard studies of helicopters for fleet and land operations. Navy helicopters performed rescues in Korea assigned to aircraft carriers, battleships, cruisers, LSTs, and British aircraft carriers. Navy helicopter detachments also target spotted for naval gunfire and searched for harbor mines. HU-2 later assumed war duty aboard ships, albeit for a brief period. Eventually, navy and marine HO3S-1s were replaced by HTL-4s.

An H-13D of the 50th Medical Detachment in Korea stands by on the helicopter pad. *Courtesy of US Army*

The H-13 did a lot more in Korea than rescue wounded, but that is how they are remembered, especially by the image fortified by the popular television series "MASH." Their role in medical evacuation most impressed army officials, for immediately after the Korean War, specifications were drawn for a new turbine-powered medical evacuation helicopter. That helicopter—the Bell Huey—not only exceeded all expectations in the "Medevac" role, its use rapidly expanded to the extent that it became the very symbol of America's next war.

In January 1952, an H-13 pilot demonstrates techniques for loading and securing wounded to the helicopter's skid-mounted litters. The pilot's attentive audience was soldiers of the 3rd Infantry Division. The division, which was one of ten active army divisions, had arrived in Korea in September 1950, and fought until war's end in July 1953. *Courtesy of Earl Thiesen*

Although army H-13s assumed the major medevac role in Korea, Marine Observation Six (VMO-6) of the 1st Marine Division flew HTL-4s. During 1951 and 1952, the squadron lost nine HTL-4s; two to ground fire, and the remaining were operational losses. BuNo. 128633, seen here offloading wounded, was lost in August 1951. *Courtesy of US Navy*

The H-13 in Korea proved its usefulness beyond the medevac role, such as this H-13D outfitted to transport K-9s of the 26th Scout Dog Platoon, 2nd Aviation Company, 2nd Infantry Division. *Courtesy of US Army*

Since radio communication between pilot and ground troops often was not effective, loudspeakers were rigged to the helicopter. Various litter types were mounted to skids, this type incorporating a simple Plexiglas fairing to prevent the patient from suffocation due to wind and rotor wash. Sleeves attached to the fairing accommodated stretcher handles. *Courtesy of US Army*

An H-13D (s/n 51-2525) takes off with wounded from the 32nd Collecting Station of the 7th Infantry in August 1952. *Courtesy of US Army*

Given the HTL's size, there was room to spare on the deck of the USS *Valley Forge* (CVA-45) in January 1953, when the carrier transported eight HTL-3s to Korea for casualty evacuation. Although Bell test pilot Joe Mashman had demonstrated skid landing gear in November 1950, some navy HTLs, and army H-13s in Korea did not swap their wheels for skids until 1951. *Courtesy of US Navy*

CHAPTER 5
Aeroscouts

In contrast to the Korean War, in America's next war, the H-13 assumed a more aggressive role. As the US Army's primary observation helicopter during the early 1960s, the Sioux easily met the requirement for providing a battlefield reconnaissance capability. Pending the arrival of the ultimate Light Observation Helicopter (LOH)—Hughes' turbine-powered OH-6A "Cayuse," H-13 crews in Vietnam pioneered combat reconnaissance, often prodding the elusive enemy into battle. Bell H-13s, and their crews, along with Hiller H-23G "Ravens," were dubbed "Aeroscouts," which identified a key element in the Airmobile concept. That concept, which was based largely on air cavalry, grew from the army's quest to enlarge its helicopter force to coincide with the development of its tactical doctrine with helicopters.

When the decision was made to commit observation helicopters to the Vietnam conflict, the US Army possessed 861 H-13s in E, G, and H models. The first Sioux helicopters to arrive in Vietnam were assigned to the 8th and 57th Transportation Companies flying CH-21 transport helicopters. Arriving in December 1961, each company had a pair of H-13Es.

The 11th Air Assault Division, which had nine H-13s assigned when it was formed in 1963, evolved into the famed 1st Cavalry Division. Nicknamed "The First Team," the division wrote the book on Airmobile operations in Vietnam, and its Aeroscouts became legend. The First Team's vast helicopter inventory comprised 428 helicopters, sixty-four of which were H-13S models. Each air cavalry troop was assigned nine or ten H-13s.

The Aeroscout's lot was high drama and high risk as pilot-observer teams in H-13s flew low and slow to close with the enemy. To trade blows with the enemy in the high-threat environment, Aeroscouts armed themselves and their Scout helicopters. Key among their weaponry was the M60 machine gun, which hung on a strap in the observer's doorway, giving him extreme latitude for maximum coverage. A fixed version of the weapon was seen on H-13s of many air cavalry troops. Comprising one or two M60C machine guns, the M2 system was skid-mounted and controlled by the pilot. The M2 imposed a severe weight penalty and it was removed in favor of ample amounts of machine gun ammunition and grenades. Typically overloaded for combat, H-13s struggled to get into the air, made even more difficult by Vietnam's tropical climate.

Eight OH-13S helicopters of E Battery, 82nd Artillery, 1st Cavalry Division are visible at An Khe. With more than 400 helicopters due to arrive at An Khe, Camp Radcliffe, in 1965, to become home of the 1st Cavalry Division, much of the natural vegetation was retained to reduce dust, earning it the name "The Golf Course." E Battery was unique in that it operated enough OH-13Ss to attach one to each of the division's artillery batteries. Crewmen adjusted artillery fire from the air, versus from conventional ground observation posts. *Courtesy of Ed Lemp*

Since production and delivery of the Cayuse did not meet the army's requirement for 377 LOHs in Vietnam, seventy-one H-13s were moved in May 1967, from assignments in Europe to the war zone. By the end of August, 171 H-13s were sharing the Aeroscout role with 190 H-23s. Although OH-6As began arriving in October 1967, the army took delivery of 151 H-13Ss to cover losses in Vietnam.

Through attrition and replacement by OH-6As, Aeroscout H-13s eventually disappeared from the war zone by late 1969, only to return in early 1971, due to staggering OH-6A losses. Nearly 150 US Army H-13s, and their valiant crews were lost in Vietnam.

Besides US Army H-13s and a small number of Model 47s in the Vietnamese Air Force inventory, two Bell 47Gs flew for Air America affiliates during the early 1960s. Bell 47s were part of an Australian commitment named Royal Australian Air Force Independent Reconnaissance Flight 161, nicknamed "Possums." During the period of September 1965 through September 1971, 161 Recce Flight flew thirty-seven Bell 47G3B-1 helicopters in Vietnam. Armament for some of the Bells consisted mainly of M60 machine guns either pintle mounted or fixed to skids for firing by the pilot. Recce flight crews used their Model 47s for scouting, command and control, radio relay, resupply, psywar, medevac, and artillery spotting missions. Eight of 161 Recce Flight's Sioux helicopters were shot down or damaged beyond repair.

Despite combat, operational losses often accounted for aircraft losses. The pilot of this OH-13S (s/n 64-15391) escaped injury when his Sioux crashed on December 14, 1965. The OH-13S, named "DB II," belonged to E Battery, 82nd Artillery of the 1st Cavalry Division. *Courtesy of Ed Lemp*

For the Aeroscout role in Vietnam in 1966, this OH-13S of B Troop, 1st Squadron, 9th Cavalry (B /1/9), 1st Cavalry Division is armed with grenades, personal weapons, and an infantry type M60A machine gun in the observer's doorway. White phosphorus grenades are kept in a rack outside the observer's position. In the forward part of the bubble canopy is a box of C rations and a body armor panel. *Courtesy of Melvin Edwards*

An OH-13S (s/n 63-9084), one of the first S models built, of B/1/9 prepares to depart a makeshift revetment at An Lao Valley, in 1967. The Sioux's skid-mounted M2 weapon system comprising 7.62 mm machine guns was augmented by the observer's M60. *Courtesy of US Army*

Sgt. Gary Rogney of A/1/9 reloads his personal M60 and the M60Cs mounted to his OH-13S at An Khe, in 1966. Rogney was wounded on a mission when a bullet that struck him exploded a tear gas grenade, filling the cockpit, but pilot WO Clement Egonis landed the aircraft, saving Rogney's life.
Courtesy of Gary Rogney Collection

Sidearms and flak vests were tools of the trade for Aeroscout crewmen that flew the unfriendly skies of Vietnam. Here, 1st Cavalry Division crewmen pre-flight their OH-13S at An Khe in 1965. *Courtesy of Ed Lemp*

To maximize their firepower, Aeroscout crews devised numerous means of arming their Sioux helicopters. Scout pilot Frank Vanatta of Headquarters Company of the 1st Cavalry Division's 1st Brigade poses with a rocket-armed OH-13S at LZ Betty, Quang Tri, Vietnam, in 1968. The three-tube launcher was used successfully until it was discovered by a command officer, and subsequently ordered removed. *Courtesy of Frank Vanatta Collection*

At a landing zone (LZ) near the Cambodian border in 1966, a Viet Cong suspect awaits his flight out in a 1st Cavalry OH-13S. *Courtesy of Ed Lemp*

Crewmen of RAAF 161st Recce Flight in Vietnam in 1970, load an M94 40 mm grenade launcher fix-mounted in the cabin of one of the unit's 47G-3B-1 Sioux helicopters. American Aeroscout crews relied upon the hand-fired M79 40 mm grenade launcher. *Courtesy of E.T. Bevans/161st Recce Association*

"Possum" crewman John Goritchan of the Australian 161st Recce Flight demonstrates the unit's armed observer position with the M60 machine gun. The 47G-3B-1 No. 728 served in Vietnam during 1970 and 1971. *Courtesy of 161st Recce Association*

CHAPTER 6
The Global 47

Even before the Bell 47 made its mark during the Korean War, Bell Aircraft Corporation had gained recognition internationally. The first Bell design built under license abroad was the Model 48, a limited number of which were built by Italy's Costruzioni Aeronautiche Giovanni Agusta in 1948. Nations that became major operators of Model 47s were Great Britain, Italy, Spain, West Germany, Brazil, France, Australia, Israel, Columbia, and Canada. The commercial use of Model 47s in Canada is legend. America's northern neighbor was an early customer, with a 47B-3 flying over the Canadian Rockies in March 1947. This was Bell's fifth production machine, which was later evaluated by the Canadian government, leading to a Royal Canadian Air Force purchase of nine H-13s, the first of which arrived in 1948. In September 1950, the Royal Canadian Navy formed its first helicopter unit with Model 47s.

By 1953, when Bell introduced its Model 47G, and when the 1,000th Model 47 rolled off the production line, most of the free countries of the world were flying Model 47s in commercial and military capacities, and at all levels of government. Proven as a safe and practical aircraft, the Model 47 was universally accepted as a valuable tool for countless tasks.

In 1954, Agusta secured license to produce Model 47s, the first of which was delivered to the Italian Air Ministry. Among the numerous models produced by Agusta was a torpedo-armed anti-submarine warfare (ASW) version of the 47J-3 for the Italian navy. Also popular were high altitude 47G-3B-1s for Italy's air force. The firm produced more than 1,200 Model 47s of all types before production ended in 1976. When selection of a new trainer helicopter for the Italian military was delayed during the 1970s, ex-US Army H-13s were purchased from a scrap yard and rebuilt.

Also under license, the Nippon Machinery Trading Company delivered its first Model 47 to the Japanese National Security Force in 1954. In July of that year, the force was reorganized into ground, maritime, and air self-defense forces. Kawasaki Heavy Industries then assumed licensing and began deliveries of 47G-2s, and 47G-2As to the Japanese military. The firm later produced 47Js, and in 1967, developed the KH-4, which was derived from the 47G-3B. The KH-4 featured a redesigned, four-seat cabin with revised instrument layout, a modified control system, and larger fuel capacity.

Records documenting this Bell 47D have proven difficult to locate, nevertheless, it wears Brazilian registry. *Author's Collection*

The government that operated the largest number of Model 47s outside the US was that of Great Britain, where licensed production of the type by Westland Aircraft Ltd. at Yeovil began in 1964. Westland retained the Sioux name for its 422 machines, 253 of which were 47G-3B-1s, re-designated AH Mk.1s for the British Army. Other variants were dual-control AT Mk.1 and Mk.2 produced under a complex licensing agreement between Westland and Sikorsky not to produce a rival US helicopter. The first fifty Sioux were built by Agusta with deliveries beginning in April 1964. Besides several army units, two military demonstration teams—the Tomahawks and the Blue Eagles—flew the Westland Sioux. Westland production of the Sioux ended in December 1969, with the last sixteen machines sold into Germany's commercial aviation. After the British Army Air Corps began retiring older airframes in 1970, many Sioux passed into private ownership in Germany and Great Britain.

The pilot training school of West Germany's *Luftwaffe* received its first 47G-2 in 1957, with forty-five G-2s eventually in service until 1974. Fourteen were Bell-produced, and thirty-one were Agusta-built. Spain was a major customer, having operated fifty-six Model 47s for its army, navy, and air force. The Spanish Naval Air Service was resurrected in February 1954 with three 47G-2s supplied under the US Military Assistance Program. The Spanish

Navy acquired nine additional Model 47s, while the remainder for the army and air force were evenly divided between Agusta 47G-2/-3Bs, and Bell H-13H/Ss. Before Spanish military Model 47s ceased operations in 1987, they were re-designated Z.7A/Bs.

The government of Brazil took delivery of nearly seventy Model 47s, beginning in 1953 with a trio of 47D-1s for the Brazilian Air Force (FAB). The largest number of Model 47s included twelve H-13Gs, and thirty-six H-13H for the FAB, with deliveries beginning in 1959. Five H-13Js served the FAB from 1958 to 1974. Eight served the navy from 1958 to 1968, which were Kawasaki-built 47Gs and the remainder 47Js. Argentina's navy became the first naval air arm in South America to operate helicopters when, in May 1949, a Bell 47D made its first flight. By the end of that year, six 47Ds were flying from naval base Punta Indio. Nearly thirty Model 47s in six variants went to the Columbian Air Force (FAC) between 1954 and 1961.

The French air force, army, navy, and Gendarmerie flew a mix of more than 150 Model 47s. More than forty were 47Gs, with 110 built by Agusta. Deliveries of 47D-1s to France's naval air arm began in 1951. When the army retired the Model 47 in 1965, a number of them were transferred to Israel's Army Aviation. French Agusta 47s saw widespread use in the war in Algeria.

The Israeli Air Force (IAF) took on a helicopter capability in September 1965 with formation of its Second Helicopter Squadron equipped with thirteen Bell 47Gs, and Agusta 47G-2s obtained from the French Air Force. In 1966, the Model 47s were tested for the medevac role, and for anti-tank assault, armed with SS-10 missiles, rockets, and machine guns. During the June 1967 Six Day War, the Model 47s, along with Alouette IIs, flew observation and resupply missions. The 47Gs, with tank battalion commanders aboard, flew only a few feet off the desert floor, allowing them to scout Arab tanks and direct Israeli tanks across treacherous terrain to catch the Arabs by surprise. After the war and a fatal crash, the IAF concluded that the Model 47s were suitable for training but not well suited for missions, and the remaining dozen were sold, six of them to Iran.

Following a post-World War II venture by Bell and Kawasaki Heavy Industries of Japan, production of Bell 47s in Japan began in 1952. This H-13E, serialed H-3006, of the Japanese Self-Defense Force (JSDF), 4th Division Headquarters participates in a training exercise at Korala, Kyushu, Japan, in March 1955. Racks for five-gallon jerry cans were affixed to both sides of the aircraft. *Author's Collection*

Beginning in 1956, the French air force, army, navy, and Gendarmerie took delivery of approximately forty Bell 47Gs, and 110 Agusta 47Gs. Most were withdrawn from use by 1965, with some transferred to Israel. *Author's Collection*

This was the first-produced Kawasaki KH-4 seen here displayed at Johnson Air Force Base in 1967. Based on the Bell 47G-3B, the KH-4 had a maximum takeoff weight of 2,850 pounds, and a top speed of 105 mph. The aircraft wears markings of the JGSDF. *Courtesy of Nick Williams*

The Italian government made widespread use of Agusta Bell 47s. This 47J served the Guardia di Finanza (GdF), which is a law enforcement agency responsible for dealing with financial crime and smuggling. As a military force, the GdF operates a massive maritime fleet and more than 100 aircraft to patrol Italy's territorial waters. *Author's Collection*

Painted overall silver, this Agusta Bell 47G-2 features a sliding window modification in 1983. *Courtesy of Massimo Gori*

An Agusta Bell 47J of the Italian Air Force. Tail rotors were painted the national colors. *Author's Collection*

Among the line of 47G and 47J models built by Giovanni Agusta was the high altitude 47G-3B-1, such as this example (mm 80487) of the Italian Air Force, seen here at Bolzano, in August 1983. *Author's Collection*

West Germany's Luftwaffe took delivery of forty-five Model 47G-2s, with the first machine arriving in 1957; thirty-one were built by Agusta, and the remaining fourteen by Bell. Most were used as pilot trainers, while others served the West German Army, and the German Federal Border Police. Number 74 21, seen here in 1973, like most German military 47G-2s, was sold into private ownership. *Author's Collection*

By the 1960s, Autair Helicopter Services, Inc. of Canada, was operating eighteen Bell 47s. As an international firm, Autair leased some 47s in Germany for agricultural work. This 47G in 1968 wore the company colors white and medium blue. *Author's Collection*

Japan's Maritime Self-Defense Force (JMSDF) took delivery of eight Kawasaki 47G-2As. Serial number 8751 was first of the batch, which wore markings indicating service in the Arctic. Introduced in 1961, Kawasaki built thirty-three 47G-2As, while fifty-one were built by Bell. The 47G-2A was an improvement of the G-2, having a lengthened tail boom and larger rotor system. *Author's Collection*

The Brazilian Air Force (FAB) began flying Model 47s in 1953, eventually acquiring nearly seventy of the type, including serial number 8512, which was one of five 47Js of the FAB. *Courtesy of Sergio Luis Dos Santos*

A Swiss registered Model 47 Soloy turbine-powered conversion in 1990. Its red-yellow scheme was effective in Switzerland's snowy terrain. *Courtesy of Markus Herzig*

The 47G-2 was a 1955 development of a more powerful version of the 47G using a 260 hp Lycoming engine for high altitude, hot weather operations. This Agusta 47G-2 of the Spanish Air Force is seen at Madrid in 1975. Livery was overall dark green with serial no. HE.7A-50, and a St. Andrews Cross, plus FAMET eagle badge on the ventral fin. *Author's Collection*

A Bell 47G of the Indonesian Air Force 7 Training Squadron at Kalijati Air Force Base, in 2000. *Courtesy of Bottaro Sergio*

Serial number A-056 was one of seven Model 47s of Uruguay's navy. The service began using Bell 47s in 1955 until they were retired in 1996. This example was based at Laguna del Sauces in 1995. In the background is a Grumman S-2. *Courtesy of Jack Friell*

This 47G was assigned to the training wing of the Hellenic Air Force. It was one of thirteen 47G-5s delivered to Greece's air force, along with six 47G-3B-2s. The 47G-5 was introduced in 1965 as a low cost workhorse with maximum fuel loads. The color scheme was gray and blue. *Author's Collection*

This colorfully marked aircraft is believed to be one of the RAF Central Flying School's three HT Mk.2s that formed the demonstration flying team "Tomahawks" from 1967 to 1969. The team's star performance was for the RAF's 50th Anniversary Review at RAF Abingdon, Oxfordshire in 1968. *Author's Collection*

In 1965, thirteen Model 47G-3B-1s and -2s began service with the New Zealand Air Force. In 1993, five of the remaining Sioux were assigned to No. 3 Squadron at Auckland where they continued to provide helicopter conversion training. Serial number 3710 is seen here in pristine condition in 1984. *Author's Collection*

Among the small air force of the independent state of South Africa is the Defence Force Air Wing flying this Soloy Bell 47G. The mint condition classic is considered a treasure, and is one of the last Model 47s flown by a military unit. *Courtesy of Giorgio Ciarini*

The British Army Air Corps has a long history of Westland-built Sioux helicopters, as well as those built by Agusta during the 1960s. Equipped with a searchlight, this Sioux (XT819) flew with Britain's Army Air Corps until it was retired in 1976. *Author's Collection*

A Kawasaki KH-4 of Osaka Airways, in 1969. *Author's Collection*

In standard Royal Australian Army scheme, this 47G-3B-1 was equipped with large equipment containers. Seen at Richmond, Australia, in May 1967, this Sioux later would wear a large white "ARMY" title on its fuel tanks and the serial A1-405 would appear on the ventral fin. *Courtesy of Ian Macpherson*

The Helicopter Flight, Malta Land Force was established in May 1972, with three Agusta 47G-2s donated by the West German government, along with a Bell 47G-2. This machine served the Luftwaffe serialed 74 20. Under a 2000 designation system for Armed Forces Malta (AFM), this 47G-2 became AS 7203 with "AS" denoting Air Squadron, "72" the year acquired, and "03" meaning the third acquisition of the type. On its fuel tanks are AFM crests. AS 7203 was sold to a British firm in 1997. *Courtesy of Emiel Sloot*

A Westland Bell 47G-3B-1 of the Royal Australian Army in 1972.
Courtesy of Peter Keating/Jack Friell Collection

A superb detail view taken by Wal Nelowkin of Westland Bell 47G-3B-1 (A1-396) of the Royal Australian Army.

A CH-13G of the Canadian Navy at Rockcliffe, in June 1967. In the background with folded wings is a Hawker Sea Fury FB 11. Common to aircraft of the Royal Canadian Navy were three-digit pennant numbers. *Courtesy of Nelson Hare*

A Bell Model 47G-5A of the Swedish Police Wing in 1972. *Author's Collection*

The Canadian Coast Guard has a long history of Bell Model 47s, up to the 47J Ranger before replacement by Bell Model 206s. All wore the high visibility white and red scheme. This Model 47G (C-FDTR) rests on the helicopter pad at Kitsilano Point, Vancouver, British Columbia, in 1978. *Author's Collection*

From 1954 to 1961, the Columbian Air Force (FAC) took delivery of 27 Model 47s of various types. This colorful 47G-3B poses with a de Havilland DHC-2 Beaver at Medellin-Rionegro Airport, in 2008. The 47G-3B was assigned as a trainer aircraft at Columbia's Melgar base. Both aircraft wear Columbia's national colors on their tail fins. *Courtesy of Andres Ramirez*

This is one of six Bell 47D-1s flown by No. 333 Squadron of the Royal Norwegian Air Force (RNAF), from 1953 to 1971. The RNAF also operated three Model 47G-3s during that time frame. *Author's Collection*

Respendent in its high-visibility training scheme of orange and white, this 47G-3B-1 (XT146) was among the first batch of fifty Sioux built for the Royal Air Force by Agusta at Gallerate, Italy. In RAF service, this trainer was designated HT.Mk.2 and assigned to RAF Central Flying School (CFS) at Ternhill, in 1965. RAF interest in the Army Air Corps Sioux led to a contract for fifteen HT.Mk.2s. The Mk.2 served the CFS until 1973, when it was replaced by the Gazelle. *Author's Collection*

This is one of nine Model 47G and G-2As operated by the Chilean navy. This G-2 used older style skid gear but featured a widened canopy over previous models. The G-2's 260hp Lycoming VO-435 engine proved essential in Chile's hot and high regions. *Courtesy of Bell Helicopter*

Beginning in 1965, the Peruvian Air Force (FAP) took delivery of thirty Model 47Gs, which were a mix of models G, 3B-1, 3B-2, and G-5A. The 47G-3B-1 seen here was the second in service with FAP Helicopter Group 3 at Callao. This model featured the largest bubble canopy of the 47 series, along with the longest tail boom and main rotors. *Courtesy of Bell Helicopter*

The RAF Blue Eagles flew five Westland Bell Sioux AH.1s at Army Air Corps School of Aviation at Middle Wallop, Hants, from 1968 to 1975. *Author's Collection*

CHAPTER 7
Special Projects

Besides modification programs and experiments common to any aircraft that enjoyed a long production run, certain projects in the Model 47's history merit special attention. When US Army experiments with armed helicopters began in earnest in 1962, Bell proposed a gunship design called "Warrior," along with its Model 207 "Sioux Scout," which embodied components of several Model 47 variants. A refined 47J-2 rear fuselage, tail boom, and transmission were mated with a streamlined, tandem cockpit featuring side-arm controls for the gunner who sat in front. A supercharged Lycoming 220 hp piston engine powered the modified tail rotor and thirty-seven-foot diameter main rotor that came from the OH-13S. Several wing designs were evaluated on the Sioux Scout to assist with lift, carry extra fuel, and to provide ordnance mounts. Muscle for the Scout consisted of an Emerson Electric turret housing a pair of 7.62 mm machine guns.

The Model 207 first flew on June 27, 1963, and later that year underwent evaluation by the 11th Air Assault Division, forerunner of the famed 1st Cavalry Division, and pioneers of the Airmobile concept. Army evaluators were impressed with all aspects of the Sioux Scout, but found its insufficient power a glaring drawback for an attack helicopter. Bell acted on their recommendation for turbine power, and refined the design to produce the awesome line of Hueycobra gunships.

Speaking of turbine power, also in 1963 Bell engineers mated a pair of navy HUL-1s with turbine engines resulting in re-designation HUL-1M, which was changed to UH-13R (BuNo. 149838 and 149839). The army-funded program was aimed at testing first an Allison T63 engine for the three competitors of the light observation helicopter (LOH) program, followed by tests of the alternate 250 shp T65 turbine engine.

Among the many test versions of the Model 47 built during the late 1950s and early 1960s, was another winged helicopter, also built in 1963. A 47G-2 (N6723D) called "Wing Ding" was fit with fixed wings and was intended to enable the aircraft to carry loads heavier than it could lift from a hover. Wing Ding left the ground but the concept did not. It was returned to its original configuration and sold into private ownership.

By 1961, Bell engineers had developed rigid rotor, or hingeless rotor, technology to the extent that it could be applied throughout the range of rotary-wing aircraft. The study and flight test of rigid rotor, which was intended to replace the articulated single rotor,

began at Bell in 1957. Rigid rotor testing dates back to 1939, however, results were unfavorable due to non-existing technology and failure to build flexibility into the system to alleviate component stress. Bell shared rigid rotor research with Lockheed Aircraft Corporation and NASA, however, to provide research information only. Lockheed's interest was for development of an operational rigid rotor aircraft.

The Model 47 played a major role in the test with a number of variants serving as test platforms. Chief among them was an H-13G loaned from the army to NASA's Langley Research Center. Tests conducted with the H-13G from 1960 to 1963, showed marked improvement in controllability and flying qualities. Center of gravity travel was nearly unlimited. Rotor hub drag was substantially reduced as was maintenance, thanks largely to less parts and simpler operation. The system, simply put, rigidly fastened the rotor hub to the mast, with the only bearings being in the rotor blade pitch change mechanism; independent tilting familiar to Bell's conventional rotor was eliminated.

Since 1949, more than twenty Model 47s have been operated at NASA facilities. Besides HTL-6s used to train astronauts, other Model 47s contributed to the space program. During late 1967, Bell delivered to NASA three Lunar Landing Training Vehicles (LLTV) for the Apollo program. Powered by a massive turbofan engine plus twenty-four rockets, the two-ton machine incorporated Model 47 cockpit and canopy sections. One LLTV was destroyed in a crash in December 1968, and several astronauts flew the remaining pair into the late 1980s.

Today's Bell/Boeing V-22 "Osprey" is an outgrowth of Bell's involvement with tilt-rotor aircraft that dates back to 1950 when a design competition was announced for development of a convertiplane for the army. Such an aircraft had great potential in terrain that ruled out fixed-wing aircraft. Foreshadowing Bell's interest in tilt-rotor technology was inventor Arthur Young's 1941 design of a combination helicopter-airplane patented in 1945. Nevertheless, Bell Aircraft Corporation shared the credit for the first-built tilt wing model with Vertol Aircraft Corporation. Noteworthy, is the fact that Vertol's design was built around a Model 47 airframe with a complete cockpit. Developed for the army and Office of Naval Research (ONR), the Vertical Takeoff and Landing (VTOL) aircraft, designated Vertol 76, or VZ-2, accomplished the first complete conversion flight on July 15, 1958. By contrast, the Bell-designed XV-3 convertiplane made its first complete flight transition five months later. Transition from hover to forward flight and back to landing was accomplished by tilting the entire wing with rotor-propellers from vertical to horizontal. After accomplishing a number of breakthroughs in tilt-wing technology, the Vertol 76 was relegated to the Smithsonian Institution.

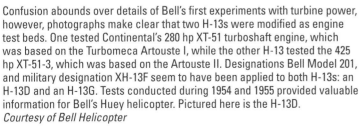

Confusion abounds over details of Bell's first experiments with turbine power, however, photographs make clear that two H-13s were modified as engine test beds. One tested Continental's 280 hp XT-51 turboshaft engine, which was based on the Turbomeca Artouste I, while the other H-13 tested the 425 hp XT-51-3, which was based on the Artouste II. Designations Bell Model 201, and military designation XH-13F seem to have been applied to both H-13s: an H-13D and an H-13G. Tests conducted during 1954 and 1955 provided valuable information for Bell's Huey helicopter. Pictured here is the H-13D. *Courtesy of Bell Helicopter*

The data block of this H-13G identifies it as XH-13F with serial number 52-7974, along with an Artouste engine number and an air force contract number. Engine manufacturer records indicate that this H-13 tested the XT-51-3 engine. *Courtesy of Bell Helicopter*

Loaned by the army to NASA for rigid rotor flight test from 1960 to 1963, this H-13G first was flown with three eleven-inch chord blades, and later with eight-inch chord blades. The synchronized elevator was removed since the system so improved flying qualities that no stabilization device or tail surfaces were required. The H-13G retained its army markings, minus the serial number, and NASA emblems were applied to the fuel tanks. *Courtesy of NASA*

The rotor hub of the three-blade rigid rotor test H-13G. The system used a less complex hub that included vertical linkage only for rotating blades to change pitch angle. Flight test instrumentation focused on rotor hub component stress. The long flex tube is the carburetor air intake. *Courtesy of NASA*

In 1967, Bell's LLTV (Lunar Landing Training Vehicle) replaced the LLRV (Lunar Landing Research Vehicle) also built by Bell during the early 1960s. The LLTV first flew at Ellington Air Force Base on October 3, 1968, prior to astronaut training to simulate landing on the moon. The vehicle's horizontal speed was sixty feet per second and it could climb at thirty feet per second. A total of twenty-four rockets of various types and thrusts were used for thrust boost, attitude control, and in the event of engine failure. *Courtesy of NASA*

Over the years, NASA operated more than twenty Model 47s of various types at its facilities. This Model 47G-3B-2, registered NASA 949, is seen here in 1978. *Author's Collection*

An early 1960s configuration of the Vertol 76 with larger cockpit fabricated from a Bell 47, and an advanced wing design. The names of eleven test pilots appear on the cockpit door. *Courtesy of Boeing Vertol*

Billed by Vertol Aircraft Corporation as the first tilt-wing model ever built, the Vertol 76 was built around a Bell Model 47 airframe with complete cockpit and familiar bubble canopy. Initially a classified project, it was developed for the army and Office of Naval Research. Shown in April 1957 are the wing positions for helicopter-like takeoff and landing, and for forward flight. *Courtesy of US Army*

The Scout's copilot/gunner cyclic was a side-arm control. It replaced the pedals by turning cyclic grip to control yaw. Bell pilot Ned Gilliand said that flying in the rear seat was like flying a heavy Model 47. Pedals could not be used in the front cockpit as they would interfere with the gunner's entrance and egress, and they would impede the floor-mounted gun sight. *Courtesy of Bell Helicopter*

In 1963, the Model 207 was tested with various wing styles after undergoing ground tests without wings. Since the 207 was a secret project, it was painted white to avert attention from its role as a gunship demonstrator. *Courtesy of Ned Gilliand Collection*

Bell's Model 207 was an in-house project, seen here in early stages of development, minus weapon systems and without a vertical fin.
Courtesy of Ned Gilliand Collection

The Sioux Scout's gunner/copilot accessed the cockpit through a hinged canopy and collapsible gunsight. The design pioneered the use of armchair flight controls, along with the TAT-101 dual 7.62 mm machine gun turret.
Courtesy of Ned Gilliand Collection

Developed during 1963, "Wing Ding" investigated the possibilities of combining the agility of the helicopter with the load-lifting capabilities of the airplane. It was powered by a standard Lycoming VO-435 engine, and the rotor mast could be tilted during flight to increase speed. Wing Ding's wings spanned twenty-five feet and carried fifteen-gallon fuel tanks inboard; later these were added onto the wing tips. A tail skid was added to protect the oversize ventral fin. Wing Ding was painted white with a red ventral fin, fuel tanks, wing tips, elevators, and cabin belly panel. "Wing Ding" appeared in gold above the registration. *Courtesy of Bell Helicopter*

Listed first is the commercial designation, followed by the US Army/US Air Force designation, and then the US Navy/US Marine Corps designations. Diligent research shows that sources available, including those obtained from dated Bell archives, often contradict model designations, their histories, and the exact numbers produced. More accurate documentation exists for military serials and bureau numbers.

Model 30	three prototypes, flight testing began in 1942 (NX41867, NX41868, and NX41869).
47	1945 debut, third Model 30 became prototype, ten additional built for tests.
47A/YR-13/HTL-1	twenty-eight built (S/N 46-227/254), three YR-13 (S/N 46-228/230) modified in 1947 for cold weather tests in Alaska—re-designated YH-13A in 1948, ten allocated to US Navy as HTL-1s (S/N 46-236, 237, 242/244, 249/251, 253, 254), two of these later transferred to US Coast Guard.
47B	first production variant, 175 hp Franklin engine, two-place, seventy-eight built.
47B-2	one experimental machine.
47B-3	agricultural use, thirty-three built.
47D/H-13B/HTL-2	fully enclosed canopy with convertible option, float gear option, sixty-seven built, sixty-five H-13Bs with 200 hp Franklin engine built for a US Army order (S/N 48-796/860—army technical orders dated 1955 and 1957 label these serials as H-13C), in 1950 one H-13B was modified to YH-13C by removing rear fuselage and tail boom covering, fit with skid landing gear incorporating ground handling wheels and litters, tail rotor guard, and ventral fin, in 1951 and 1952 sixteen more were built, having serials 48-799/800, 804/806, 808, 810/812, 824/828, 835/837 and 848), twelve went to US Navy as HTL-2s (BuNo. 122952/122963).
47D-1/H-13D/HTL-3/HTL-4	one-piece canopy, increased payload, exposed tail boom, twenty-nine-gallon gravity-feed fuel tank, eighty-seven built as H-13D (S/N 51-2446/2531, 51-17669), nine built as HTL-3 for US Navy (BuNo. 124561/124569), sixty built for US Navy as HTL-4 (BuNo. 128621/128636, 128887/128916), twelve later were passed to the US Marine Corps for squadrons HMX-1 and VMO-6.

HTL-5	basically identical with the HTL-4 but having an improved transmission, thirty-six built for US Navy (BuNo. 129942/129977), both HTL-4 and -5 were re-designated TH-13Ls in 1962.
47E/H-13E/HTL-3	one experimental model 47E built in 1950, 553 H-13E built including S/N 51-13742/14231 for US Army, nine to US Navy as HTL-3 (BuNo. 124561/124569).
47F	built in 1951 as a three-place, general purpose helicopter, designation XH-13F given to two H-13s—an H-13D and an H-13G (S/N 52-7974)—that served as test beds for turbine engines during mid-1950s.
47G/H-13G/HTL-6	introduced in 1953, twin fuel tanks, synchronized elevator, widened canopy, float option, 208 built, 265 H-13Gs built for US Army, one transferred to US Navy which led to an order for forty-six HTL-6s, which were re-designated TH-13M in 1962, production by Agusta began in 1954, twenty-four built by Kawasaki.
47G-1	one experimental model built (N2474B) as proof-of-concept machine, prototype for 47J model.
47G-2/H-13H	production of the 47G-2 Trooper began in 1955 with 334 built, 260 hp Lycoming engine, introduced arched skid cross tubes, delivery of 470 H-13Hs to US Army began in 1956, 304 built by Agusta and 180 by Kawasaki.
47G-2A	introduced in 1960, 220 hp Lycoming engine, redesigned rotor head, fifty-one built, thirty-three by Kawasaki.
47G-2A-1	widened cockpit, increased fuel capacity, twenty-five built.
47G-3/H-13K	introduced in 1959, 225 hp turbocharged Franklin engine, rotor diameter increased by twelve inches and tail boom lengthened by fourteen inches, high altitude performance, deliveries of the Trooper began in 1960, thirty-eight built, H-13K identified two H-13H (59-4971/4972) modified with 225 hp engine for US Army high altitude tests, 59-4971 later transferred to USN.
47G-3B/OH-13S	introduced in 1961, 260 hp turbo-supercharged Lycoming engine, three-place, gross weight 2,850 lbs, eighty built, 265 OH-13S built for US Army, 210 built by Kawasaki as KH-4.
47G-3B-1/TH-13T	270 hp Lycoming engine, three-place cabin widened by eight inches, high-inertia rotor, improved controls, maximum gross weight increased to 2,950 lbs, older style skid gear, 330 built, 411 TH-13T built for US Army trainer with tinted canopy and additional avionics with deliveries beginning in 1964, Westland produced 253 as Sioux AH Mk.1 and HT Mk.2 for British Army.
47G-3B-2	introduced in 1968, 280 hp supercharged Lycoming engine, fuel capacity increased to fifty-seven gallons, cabin widened to five feet, 158 built, also produced by Agusta.
47G-4	Trooper was a 1964 model with 305 hp Lycoming engine, eighty-six built.
47G-4A	introduced in 1965, 280 hp engine, 268 built, fifty-nine built by Agusta.

47G-5	low cost, three-place utility model introduced in 1965, 265 hp, 184 built.
47G-Ag-5	two-seat agricultural version of G-5 offered same year, two sixty-gallon hoppers and spray booms, 336 built including those by Agusta.
47H	Bellairus, 47H and 47H-1 designations used interchangeably, 1955 deluxe version of 47G, 200 hp Franklin engine, metal covered tail boom with luggage compartment, three-place leather soundproofed interior, thirty-three built.
47J/H-13J/HUL-1, HUL-1G	Ranger series introduced in 1955, is a modified G model with metal-covered streamlined tail boom with larger cabin to accommodate three passengers on bench seat behind pilot, or two stretchers and attendant, plus a door for installation of an electric hoist, 220 hp Lycoming engine, maximum speed of 105 mph, maximum gross weight 2,565 lbs, metal rotor blade option, 135 built, twenty-eight HUL-1 with 240 hp engines and hoists built for USN squadrons HU-1 and HU-2, in 1962 HUL-1 re-designated UH-13P, two transferred from USN order to US Coast Guard as HUL-1Gs re-designated HH-13Qs in 1962, Agusta built 152, two were specially built as VH-13J for President Eisenhower and later re-designated UH-13J (57-2728/2729).
47J-1	sub-variant of the 47J powered by an improved Lycoming VO-435A engine.
47J-2	1960 Ranger was a streamlined version of the 47J with 260 hp Lycoming engine, hydraulic controls, and metal rotor blades, three versions were utility, four-place executive, and cargo, 103 built.
47J-2A	four-place executive transport with 260 hp Lycoming engine, introduced in 1964, seventy-five built, also built by Agusta.
47J-3	Super Ranger introduced in 1965 with 260 hp engine and strengthened transmission, Agusta built 123 of -2 and -3 models including ASW version for Italian Navy.
47J-3B-1	1965, 270 hp, 123 Agusta-built as -1, -2, and -3 versions.
47K/HTL-7	smaller version of 47J Ranger, eighteen HTL-7 ordered in 1957 built with HUL-1 airframe with 240 hp Lycoming engine, two-place, all-weather primary and instrument trainer for US Navy, two were diverted to USCG for assignment to ice-breakers, in 1962, HTL-7 was re-designated TH-13N.
47L/HUL-1M	proposed Ranger general purpose aircraft with two built similar to HUL-1 for US Navy (BuNo. 149838/839), re-designated UH-13R in 1962, in 1963 modified to test T63 turbine engine, HUL-1M superseded HUL-2, which was a projected version of HUL-1 powered by 250 hp Allison T-63 turbine engine.